The Battle of Middleton Cheney

6th May 1643

By Gregg Archer

Published by Northamptonshire Battlefields Society,
in association with the Battlefields Trust

First published 2023 by The Northamptonshire Battlefields Society

© The Northamptonshire Battlefields Society and the Battlefields Trust

All rights reserved. No part of this book may be reprinted or reproduced or utilised in any form or by any electronic, mechanical or other means, now known or hereafter invented, including photocopying or in any information storage or retrieval system, without the written permission of the author.

Gregg Archer has asserted his moral right to be identified as the author of this work in accordance with the Copyrights, Design and Patents Act 1988.

Cover photograph © Graham Evans.

ISBN 9798849687179

**In memory of Nicholas Haynes,
a passionate advocate for the history of his village.**

Acknowledgements

I am grateful to Nicholas Haynes, to whose memory this book is dedicated, for all his support and encouragement in the initial stages of researching the battle. At Middleton Cheney, I wish to acknowledge the help and support of Ulrika Haynes, Barney Haynes, Nicholas Leggett and Nigel Wadlow. I wish to express my gratitude to Nancy Long, the village archivist, for her assistance in the local aspects and to Nick Allen for providing the information on Warkworth. I am indebted to Nick Lipscombe for producing two of the maps in this work and for his insights in many a time walking across the battlefield and local area. At Northampton, Graham Evans, Chair of the Northamptonshire Battlefields Society, for proposing the book and his assistance in the production. I would also like to thank the Society's committee for their agreement to publish. I am also indebted to Simon Marsh of the Battlefields Trust for his constant support and advice with this project. Finally, I would like to thank my wife and children, who have been in the company of battlefields for many a year. I appreciate their support and understanding!

Preface

The battle of Middleton Cheney was not unknown to the Northamptonshire Battlefields Society and is included in our book "The Battles and Battlefields of Northamptonshire". However, with the state of knowledge at the time the book was written it received barely a paragraph, let alone a chapter, to itself. Information was scarce, not helped by the disappearance of an important primary source from the British Library shortly after it was consulted by a local antiquarian in the early 19th century.

In more modern times a project to commemorate the battle was started by Nicholas Haynes, a local Middleton Cheney resident and military historian. Gregg Archer of the Battlefields Trust was tasked with undertaking the research and despite the issues noted with sources has put together a convincing narrative of the circumstances, campaign and battle that occurred in May 1643. In doing so he has also uncovered further information about the garrison of the town of Northampton in the early stages of the Civil War.

When Gregg joined the Society, he shared with me a short pamphlet in electronic format that he was working on that had expanded from a two page article, covering the battle. Given the Society's experience of publishing books on the county's battles, it seemed an obvious step for us to offer to help prepare and publish the book to go along with our books on the battles of Northampton and Edgcote. Producing a publication together with the Battlefields Trust is a new venture for us in the Northamptonshire Battlefields Society, and one we are very excited to be involved with. The Society is very grateful for the help and support it receives from the Trust's Mercia Region, and sees the partnership between the national battlefield heritage body and local groups as essential in helping to preserve our battlefield heritage.

Graham Evans
Chair
Northamptonshire Battlefields Society.

Contents

Introduction	1
The Road to Civil War and the Edgehill campaign, 1639-1642	5
The campaigns in the Midlands, December 1642 to May 1643	10
Armies and weapons during the Civil War	15
The opposing armies - the Royalist brigade	21
The opposing armies - Parliament's force from Northampton	27
Banbury and Middleton Cheney in 1643	34
The Approach to Battle	39
The Earl Counterattacks	49
The Main Engagement	53
The Aftermath	61
Appendix - Extracts from Primary Sources	68
Bibliography	75
Commemorating the battle	81
The Battlefields Trust	82
Northamptonshire Battlefields Society	83

Illustrations

1. King Charles I (r.1625-49)
2. A romanticised view of the 2nd Earl of Northampton just before his death at the Battle of Hopton Heath
3. An infantry block deployment from Robert Streeter's map of Naseby
4. Cavalry deployment from Robert Streeter's map of Naseby
5. A contemporary illustration of a cavalry engagement
6. A gun crew with their artillery piece
7. James Compton, 3rd Earl of Northampton
8. Warkworth Castle
9. The grave slab of Sir Philip Holman
10. Banbury Lane
11. The ford at Bodicote during a dry season
12. The Parsontide Way near the battlefield
13. The floodplain from near the ford at Bodicote
14. The view towards the initial Royalist position on the ridge at Bodicote
15. The view towards Warkworth and Middleton Cheney from the ridge at Bodicote
16. A view of the battlefield from the Royalist forming up position
17. The Parliamentarian position at the top of the slope
18. Part of the battlefield viewed from the Parliamentarian position in the Town Field
19. The Town Field adjacent to Moors Drive
20. All Saints Church, Middleton Cheney
21. The entry in the parish register showing the burial of 46 soldiers the day after the battle

Maps

1. The Midlands: December 1642 - May 1643
2. Areas of control in England and Wales - May 1643
3. Middleton Cheney and Warkworth Parishes (c.1643)
4. Banbury Lane
5. The conjectural movements of the Royalist and Parliamentarian forces on 6th May 1643
6. Conjectural and alternative deployments of the Royalist and Parliamentarian forces
7. The Battle of Middleton Cheney, 6th May 1643

Tables

1. Royalist and Parliamentarian strengths at Middleton Cheney
2. Royalist and Parliamentarian casualties at Middleton Cheney

Introduction

Between 1639 and 1660, civil wars, caused by arguments between King and Parliament about the exercise of royal power, money and religion engulfed almost the entire British Isles and Ireland[1]. By the summer of 1642, King Charles I and Parliament sought a military solution to resolve their issues. The King raised an army and marched on London in October 1642, engaging Parliament's army at Edgehill later that month. Although Edgehill was, at best, a tactical draw, it left the road to London open for the Royalists. They squandered their best opportunity to end the war quickly and, at Turnham Green, were forced to withdraw to Oxford, which became their capital until its surrender in June 1646. Despite several attempts at negotiation at the county level to preserve peace, the war had escalated and by the summer of 1643 almost all of the country experienced some disturbances as King and Parliament fought to determine the balance of power within the Kingdom.

While both sides raised large field armies which marched, fought battles and laid siege to enemy-occupied towns, castles and houses, the war was also fought locally. Royalist and Parliamentarian garrisons, both large and small, were dotted around the country. These garrisons, as well as protecting the place they occupied, were used to control areas of land or supply routes which led into the main cities. The garrisons were focal points for collecting taxes, supplies, grain, animals and horses, and munitions. They served as places where the local recruits could muster before being sent to the main field armies. Rather than finding themselves in a quiet backwater, local communities were subject to taxation or extortion from small groups of soldiers. Supplies were often requisitioned or even stolen to maintain the local garrisons. Finally, villagers often found themselves burdened with troops quartered upon them. While the intention was to pay the local inhabitants, as the war progressed, they were frequently the subject of 'free quarter' and found the troops billeted among them at their own expense. When the troops were ready to depart, the villages were frequently plundered and stripped of everything from supplies to valuables.

One such garrison was Banbury at the northernmost tip of Oxfordshire, which the Royalists had captured following the battle of Edgehill and was subsequently garrisoned. Banbury soon proved to be 'the major strategic asset for the Royalists north of Oxford.'[2] The garrison, safely ensconced in the strong medieval castle, which dominated an otherwise Puritan, pro-Parliamentarian town, raided far and wide throughout Warwickshire, Northamptonshire and Oxfordshire. They were able to hinder the Parliamentarian supply line between Warwick and Gloucester and frequently captured convoys bound for the latter. Even places as far afield as Rugby and Hillmorton were subject to the extortions and raiding of the garrison.[3] As governor

---
[1] Ireland was still a Kingdom united under the Stuart dynasty with England and Scotland.
[2] Philip Tennant, *Edgehill and Beyond, The Peoples War in the South Midlands 1642-45,* (Stroud, Alan Sutton Publishing Ltd, 1992), p.77
[3] Ibid, p.77-8

of Banbury, Spencer Compton, the 2nd Earl of Northampton, was a frequent visitor, often bringing his horse regiment with him. With little space in the town, the regiment was quartered on the local inhabitants in villages such as Aynho, Kings Sutton, Bodicote, Warkworth and Middleton Cheney. The Parliamentarians depredated the area when they passed through, such as during the Earl of Essex's relief march to Gloucester in 1643, adding to the villagers' misery. Finally, the town was frequently used as a jumping-off point for Royalist campaigns in Northamptonshire and beyond. Even as early as the first year of the war, the garrison was becoming a thorough nuisance to the local Parliamentarian authorities. Colonel Nathaniel Whetham, the Parliamentarian governor of Northampton, described the garrison as a *'den of Theeves'*[4] and its activities drew, like a magnet, the attention of the local Parliamentarian commanders at Warwick and Northampton.

The first attempt to neutralise Banbury came at Christmas 1642. The garrison held firm, but the Parliamentarians were briefly able to capture the town before being driven off. The town was less secure than the castle and was occupied at least once a year by the Parliamentarians between December 1642 and the final surrender in May 1646. For the local communities, the coming and going of many troops must have placed a tremendous strain on the local economy and caused significant disruption to their everyday lives. For one community, that of Middleton Cheney, the following year was to bring their village to the forefront of the war when another Parliamentarian force from Northampton attempted to take Banbury. On Saturday, 6 May 1643, a Royalist brigade under James Compton, 3rd Earl of Northampton, clashed with this Parliamentarian force in a small action directly to the south of the village. The Parliamentarians were defeated and driven off with some loss, which temporarily removed the threat to the Royalist control in the Banbury area. Rather than seeing the soldiers come and go, the villagers experienced the direct effects of the war as the dead and dying lay in the fields around them. Finally, the war had come to Middleton Cheney.

Three hundred eighty years later, the battle again became prominent for Middleton Cheney's villagers. A local project sought to interpret and commemorate the action that, while not forgotten, showed little sign in the village that anything had happened during the civil wars. As part of this project, and in an attempt to locate the battlefield, research was commissioned, forming this book's subject.

There are few sources which fully explain the engagement in detail. On the Royalist side, only one letter written by a participant who was an officer in the Earl of Northampton's regiment has survived. Although written from a Royalist perspective and therefore almost certainly biased, it is a brief summary of the action provided to Prince Rupert, the King's nephew and commander of the Royalist Oxford Army cavalry. It does not contain the gloating, scapegoating or fault-finding of the other

---

[4] *A full Relation of the Siege of Banbury Castle by that Valiant and Faithfull Commander, Colonell Whetham, Governour of Northampton, now Commander-in-Chiefe in that Service, &c.* (BL/TT/E.8(9), London, 4 September, 1644.

accounts. There is also a brief entry in Clarendon's *History of the Great Rebellion*, written after the war when the author was in exile. There are no first-hand accounts from the Parliamentarian perspective.

We must therefore rely on the newspapers printed in London and Oxford for the remainder of our information. Here we are immediately presented with many problems. *Mercurius Aulicus*, which provides the most detailed account, was a newspaper produced in Oxford between January 1643 and September 1645. Edited by Sir John Birkenhead, the paper managed 'to dispense a concoction of facts and propaganda intended to puff up the Royalists and shrivel the adherents of Parliament.'[5] Whilst the Parliamentarian pamphlet *Mercurius Britannicus* accused *Mercurius Aulicus* of spouting nonsense and of *'things halfe made up'*, [6] with their proximity to the King's inner circle and their office in Oxford, the editors of the latter were in direct contact with the latest news. They also had access to those who fought in the battles and sieges. It was still, however, a one-sided viewpoint. Birkenhead was a master of his craft, but the selection of his news items was undoubtedly partisan. The editors even magnified minor Royalist victories to appear greater than was the case. They also used satire to ridicule their opponents and constantly sought to divide them. Royalist propaganda was initially successful due to 'its developing relationship with "serious" literary conventions; and second, its success in defining a body of viable satirical themes and images.'[7] It is against these principles that we must judge the detailed battlefield account contained in *Mercurius Aulicus*.

The London newspapers were even more prolific but were no less biased than the Oxford pamphlets. Four pamphlets that mention the battle were most concerned with delivering straight news to their readers in a rather dull and colourless fashion.[8] But all still showed a pro-Parliament bias in their writings. Indeed, they could do little else without the risk of being shut down. The Parliamentarians countered *Mercurius Aulicus'* influence by producing some of the more influential propaganda pamphlets of the war. Some, like *Mercurius Britannicus* and *The Spie*, were deliberately created to counter the Royalist newspaper but were not above fighting each other in print and accusing each other of being Royalist agents or subversives.[9] Most received their news through the letters, dispatches and proceedings in Parliament, but this intelligence was second or third-hand. Newspapers like the *Perfect Diurnall* were merely reporting letters and news already summarised in Parliament. These are not ideal sources with which to work. They are often incomplete and confused, which adds to the difficulty

---

[5] Joseph Frank, The Beginnings of the English Newspaper, 1620-1660, (Cambridge, Harvard University Press, 1961)

[6] *Mercurius Britannicus, communicating the affaires of great Britaine for the better information of the people,* Numb.70. (BL/TT/E.269 (25), London, 10 February 1645. The jibe was directed at John Cleaveland but it was clearly implied that the editor of *Mercurius Aulicus* was included.

[7] P.W.Thomas, *Sir John Berkenhead 1617-1679 A Royalist Career in Politics and Polemics,* (Oxford, Clarendon Press, 1969), p.99.

[8] Frank, *The Beginnings of the English Newspaper,* p.35-6.

[9] Thomas, p.251.

in finding clear information surrounding the nature of the fighting. There is also a great deal of detail missing and several gaps in some of these sources, making it difficult to understand the exact course of events on the ground. Many of these pamphlets are contradictory about the nature of the battle and are bereft of detailed topographical information that might help locate the battlefield itself. But that was not the point of these pamphlets. Like the Royalist periodicals, they tended to inflate victories and gloss over defeats if ever mentioned. While not ideal sources, we would have no story to tell without them.

At Middleton Cheney there is a small amount of local tradition regarding the location and reports of purported artefactual 'finds'. Oral traditions passed down through generations do not make authoritative material for constructing the narrative of a battle. The landscape may help, but pinpointing an exact location with confidence almost seems impossible without topographical detail. By pulling together these accounts, incomplete, biased and confused as they are, we can at least provide an interpretation of the events of 6 May 1643. I do not claim that the account in this publication is 'definitive'. With the available evidence, I hope I have been able to tell the story of this battle, albeit one that is open to some interpretation, to bring this often overlooked engagement to its proper place as part of the civil war history of Northamptonshire.

The Road to Civil War and the Edgehill campaign, 1639-1642

King Charles I (1600-1649) succeeded his father, James I, as King of England, Scotland and Ireland in March 1625. The new monarch was in a different mould from his father. Like James, Charles' shared belief in the divine right of kings; that kings derived their right to rule from God and were not subject to earthly authority. However whereas James took a more pragmatic approach with his views and dealings with other bodies such as Parliament and his nobles, Charles tended to be stubborn and inflexible. In the early 17th Century monarchs called Parliaments when specific political issues needed to be discussed and were not permanent sitting bodies. Foremost among these were religious and financial issues. Parliament was in session for a short period in 1625 and between February and June 1626, until its attack on Charles' favourite, the Duke of Buckingham, over his role as Lord Admiral in the failed Cadiz expedition of 1625.[1] Charles was forced to recall Parliament again in March 1628 following Buckingham's failure to capture Île de Rhé as part of an effort to support Huguenots in La Rochelle besieged by the French King. Parliament showed its unwillingness to accept the King's demands for further support for his foreign adventures. Although initially agreeing with Parliament, the King eventually dismissed it at the end of June. Parliament was recalled again in January 1629 but proved as intractable as it had been in 1628, with members holding down the speaker, Sir John Finch, to delay the session's closing.[2] The King was no less minded and dissolved Parliament in March and, for good measure, imprisoned nine Members of Parliament

Fig. 1 Charles I (r1625-1649)
(Authors Collection)

---

[1] John Kenyon, *The Civil Wars in England*, (London: Weidenfeld and Nicholson Ltd, 1988), p.10.
[2] Trevor Royle, *Civil War; The Wars of the Three Kingdoms 1638-1660*, (London, Abacus, 2005), p.23

in the process. For the next eleven years, the King called no more Parliaments and the period became known as one of 'Personal Rule'.

Given his belief in the divine right of kings, Charles saw nothing wrong in administering the country by himself with the support of his privy councillors. He soon began imposing policies simply because he thought them right and just.[3] Charles also decided to interfere in the affairs of other countries. However, in order to rule, Charles needed money and only Parliament could impose taxes. Unwilling to recall Parliament for this purpose, the King resorted to using his prerogative powers to finance his rule. These included the maintenance of existing customs duties and the imposition of new ones, the distraint of knighthood (whereby gentlemen qualified for knighthood who had refused the honour at the King's coronation were fined), fining landowners who had encroached on the limits of Royal forests, and the sale of 'patents' for new ways to make goods, creating monopolies. Famously, he also extended 'Ship Money', a charge originally instituted to help maintain the Royal Navy and levied only on maritime counties, to inland counties. Whilst there was grumbling in the maritime towns, even with their duty to maintain ships for the navy, the stream of criticism soon became a torrent when it was introduced into the inland counties. One of the most vocal critics was John Hampden, a native of Buckinghamshire, who was prosecuted and found guilty by a narrow margin of not paying the tax. The court case provided a platform for popular dissent.

Had Charles been content to confine his policies strictly to the financial, he may have been able to weather the storm, but his religious reforms also caused opposition. The King fully supported the reforms of the Anglican church proposed by Archbishop Laud but this alienated many Puritans and Presbyterians who saw these as distinctly 'Popish'. In turn, this began to fuel fears that Charles would take England back into the arms of Rome. His French wife's open practice of her Catholic religion also helped stir unrest. An attempt to introduce another Laudian reform, the 'Book of Common Prayer', into Presbyterian Scotland led to Charles' undoing. The Scottish Church (known as the Kirk) had removed many functions of the Anglican rite from their ceremonies; however, Charles wished to impose the full Anglican rite across the entirety of his three kingdoms. When Charles ordered the prayer book to be adopted in 1637, riots broke out in Edinburgh. The Scottish Church quickly reaffirmed the National Covenant, which forbade any interference in their religion without due authorisation from the Kirk and the Scottish Parliament.[4] A rebellion soon broke out, and Charles' attempts to suppress it became known as the First Bishops War. The campaign was a fiasco, and the Royal army never even managed to engage with the Covenanter forces commanded by General Alexander Leslie, a veteran of the Thirty Years War.[5] The war was short lived with Charles and the Scots agreeing in the Treaty

---

[3] C V Wedgewood, *The Kings Peace* (London, Book Club Associates, 1974), p.62. Ollard, *This war without an enemy* (Fontana Paperbacks, 1992) p.24.
[4] Wedgewood, pp.176-77.
[5] All of the fighting during the First Bishops War was in the north where the King's supporters led by George

of Berwick to disband their armies and for the King to travel to Edinburgh to conclude a settlement with the Scottish Parliament. In reality, both sides saw this as a truce whilst they rebuilt their strength for a decisive confrontation.[6]

Once again, however, Charles needed money and he recalled Parliament to this end in April 1640. Parliament's unwillingness to agree to raising taxes led the King to dissolve it the following month. Notwithstanding this, Charles decided to go to war again against the Scots. In response, the Scots army, again commanded by Alexander Leslie, invaded Northumberland. The King and Thomas Wentworth, the Earl of Strafford who was the Lord Deputy in Ireland, moved northwards to take command, but the English army under Lord Conway suffered a decisive defeat at the battle of Newburn Ford (28 August 1640). Charles managed to negotiate a truce in October, but the Scots would not retire until the English Parliament had voted peace. In the meantime, they demanded £850 daily to maintain their army. With the royal finances in a desperate state, Charles had no choice but to recall Parliament for a second time.

Consequently, the King summoned Parliament in November 1640 which later became known as the 'Long Parliament'. The now-recalled members, however, had no intention of simply voting the funds necessary to send the Scottish army home. Before they did, there were issues to address about the King's exercise of power. Opposition to Charles coalesced around John Pym, MP for Tavistock, and a Puritan who emerged as the leader of those members wishing to institute reforms. Whilst Parliament would not attack the King directly it did attack his advisors, accusing them of being his 'evil counsellors'.[7] Both the Earl of Strafford and Archbishop Laud were impeached and imprisoned and the King ultimately forced to agree to Strafford's execution.[8] Parliament demanded further reforms from the King and many of the members were suspicious, assuming the King would renege on any promises he would make at the earliest opportunity. Both sides became entrenched while the moderates in Parliament began to be wary of Pym, believing he was going far beyond what many people wanted. Charles eventually refused to surrender his power further, whilst Pym and the reformers also refused to compromise on their goals.

The flash point came in late October 1641 when the province of Ulster, in the north of Ireland, rose in rebellion. The next twelve years would see continuous warfare which became known as the Irish Confederate Wars (1641-1653). Charles and Parliament immediately realised they needed to raise an army to crush the rebellion and reassert control in Ireland. Whilst both sides agreed on this issue, there was a lack of trust regarding who should command it. Charles probably feared that Parliament would use it to force him into concessions. Pym and his supporters feared the King would use it

---

Gordon, 2nd Marquis of Huntly attempted to seize control. The only battles were at Megray Hill (15 June 1639) and the Brig O'Dee (18 June 1639)

[6] Kenyon, p.13; Maurice Ashley, *The English Civil War*, (London: Thames and Hudson, 1974); pp.14-16

[7] Most newspaper pamphlets of the day refused to attack the King directly and there are frequent references to his 'evil counsellors'. Blaming the King's advisors was one way of criticising royal policy without officially attacking the King. Surprisingly this continued throughout the First and Second Civil Wars.

[8] Royle, pp.122-127.

against them rather than the Irish rebels. Pym now brought matters to a head by introducing the 'Grand Remonstrance' into the House of Commons. The document consisted of 204 points, including 150 misdeeds of personal rule and the other 54 points as solutions to government problems. Charles, understandably, refused to accept it and also refused royal assent to the Militia Bill introduced in December, which was aimed at giving Parliament control over military force. Rather than uniting Parliament, the Grand Remonstrance split the opposition, passing by 159 votes to 148. 153 MPs did not vote for various reasons. About a third of MPs would eventually side with the King, joining his Parliament in Oxford in 1644.

In December 1641, the King was led to believe Parliament was about to impeach his wife, Queen Henrietta Maria. Fearing for her safety after the outcome of the impeachment of Strafford, Charles decided to take action and drew up charges of high treason against one of the Lords and the five most prominent opponents in the Commons. On 3 January 1642, the King swept into Parliament determined to arrest his opponents but, forewarned, they had fled before his arrival. London's citizens appeared on the streets condemning the King's breech of the privileges of Parliament and Charles retired to Hampton Court before fleeing from London to York. Once he arrived in the north, he set about rallying his supporters and in May started raising soldiers. In response Parliament used the provisions of the Militia Bill, passed in March 1642, to also establish an army. On 22 August 1642, the King raised his standard at Nottingham, a gesture which signalled his intent to challenge what he saw as his rebellious Parliament by force. The defeat of the 2nd Earl of Northampton at Southam the following day finally ended the Royalist's attempts to secure Warwickshire. The North Midlands was also unsympathetic to his cause, so Charles advanced his fledgling army from Nottingham towards the Welsh Marches.

The King arrived at Shrewsbury in early September, where he was able to recruit additional troops from Wales and the Marches. Supplies and ammunition were also obtained, and he was joined by detachments from Cheshire and the Earl of Northampton's force from the Midlands. In response, Parliament moved its newly formed army under Robert Devereux, 3rd Earl of Essex, into the Midlands. Essex installed garrisons in most of the significant towns, including Hereford, Banbury, Coventry and Warwick. Meanwhile, the main army moved on 19 September from Northampton towards Worcester, intending to block any Royalist move down the Severn Valley.[9] The Parliamentarian advance exposed Oxford, where Sir John Byron with a small cavalry force was newly arrived. The King ordered him to abandon the City and join him with as many recruits, horses and supplies as he could muster. Byron was also to bring as much of the University plate and the funds from supporters in London to help pay for the new army. Moving fast, Byron arrived at Worcester a day after Essex left Northampton. Essex and his commanders were aware of Byron's movements and attempted to cut him off at Worcester. Aware of the danger, the King

---

[9] Keith Roberts & John Tincey, *Edgehill 1642; First Battle of the English Civil War,* (Oxford, Osprey Publishing, 2001), Map, p.42.

sent Prince Rupert and the cavalry to aid Byron. On 23 September, they defeated the Parliamentarians in a minor skirmish at Powick Bridge.[10] The Royalist army left Shrewsbury on 12 October. Rather than heading south, they sidestepped Essex and moved through the Midlands via Birmingham and Kenilworth.

Essex, realising that the King was marching directly on London, left Worcester on 19 October. Advancing on a broad front, he concentrated most of his army at Alcester before continuing the pursuit of the Royalists the following day. By the evening of 22 October, Essex had arrived at Kineton with his army strung out in its quarters as far afield as Charlecote and Ilmington. The King was ahead of Essex with his quarters at Edgcote House. The Royalist army was quartered nearby at Culworth and Wormleighton. A clash near Wormleighton alerted the Royalists to the Parliamentarian presence. Essex only learned of the Royalists as they formed up the next morning on a ridge to the east of Kineton called Edgehill. The Earl then marched his forces out of Kineton and drew up to oppose the Royalists who, seeing the Parliamentarians were not going to attack, descended from the hill and deployed. The battle began with Rupert and the Royalist cavalry having spectacular success on the wings by routing the opposing horse and some of the Parliamentarian infantry. But in maintaining the pursuit, they left the field at a critical time, leaving their infantry unsupported. Essex pushed his men forward, supported by his reserve cavalry. These broke through the Royalist line and disabled the Royalist cannons. In the centre, a desperate melee almost overwhelmed the Royalist line. Only the eventual return of Rupert staved off disaster and both sides broke contact. By remaining in the field, the King claimed victory, but in reality, the battle was drawn, with no advantage gained by either side.

The strategic initiative, however, lay with Charles. Rather than a lightning dash on London, the slow progress of his army towards the capital subsequently squandered any gains he may have made. Essex, marching on a northern route, was able to arrive in London ahead of the King. Although the Royalists managed to storm Brentford, they were met at Turnham Green by an Army twice the size of their own. Realising the futility of engaging a numerically superior army, Charles retired to Oxford in early December 1642, and the City became the Royalist capital for the remainder of the war.

---

[10] Nick Lipscombe, *The English Civil War; An Atlas and concise history of the Wars of the Three Kingdoms 1639-51,* (Oxford, Osprey Publishing Ltd, 2020), p.67. Stephen Porter & Simon Marsh, *The Battle for London,* (Stroud, Amberley Publishing, 2011), p.22.

The campaigns in the Midlands, December 1642 to May 1643

The King placed his army into winter quarters on 9 December 1642. The regiments were dispersed across Oxfordshire and Buckinghamshire in several garrisons designed to protect Oxford and warn of any Parliamentarian movements in their area. The troops could also be fed and supported by their local area without burdening Oxford, which could not support such a large body of men. The garrisons included Reading, Faringdon, Brill, Wallingford and Abingdon. Three regiments, including the Earl of Northampton's foot, were dispatched to Banbury.[1] In the northern counties, Lancashire and Yorkshire saw a series of engagements in which neither side gained the upper hand. In Cornwall and Devon, despite some victories, the Royalists could also not gain any advantage. By May 1643, the Parliamentarians had chased the Royalists out of Lancashire but were defeated in Cornwall at Stratton (16 May 1643). The situation in the north began to deteriorate when the Earl of Newcastle started his campaign, which would lead to his victory in late June at Adwalton Moor.

In the Midlands, the fighting had recommenced in early February. Prince Rupert captured the town of Cirencester but could do nothing of consequence against Gloucester before being recalled to Oxford. An attempt to reinforce the Oxford Army from Wales ended in disaster in March. Lord Herbert's Welsh army managed to reach the outskirts of Gloucester, but Sir William Waller surrounded and captured it on 24 March at the Battle of Highnam. The presence of Waller in the Welsh Marches proved a significant distraction. Invading Wales, he reached as far as Usk before retiring when a small army under Prince Maurice advanced through the Forest of Dean. Waller broke out of the encirclement at Little Dean and continued to play cat-and-mouse with Maurice. Waller's success ended when, on 13 April, he was defeated at Ripple Field.[2] Retiring to Gloucester, Waller soon advanced to the northwest and captured Hereford until he was recalled to aid the Parliamentarians in Devon.

In the disputed counties of Oxfordshire, Warwickshire and Staffordshire, Parliament was keen to make inroads into the Royalist-held territory. At Banbury, the fighting had recommenced before the end of 1642. When most of the regiments quartered there were withdrawn to Oxford, the Northamptonshire forces took the opportunity to launch their first foray into the Banbury area. On 23 December, a party under the command of Sir John Norwich captured the town and besieged the garrison in the castle. The Earl of Northampton, rushing to the relief of the castle, was embarrassingly defeated at a skirmish in Deddington. Only the approach of Prince Rupert forced the Parliamentarians to withdraw.[3] Once the Prince had retired again to

---

[1] Keith Roberts, *First Newbury 1643, The turning point,* (Oxford, Osprey Publishing Ltd, 2003), p.9.
[2] John Corbet, *A true and impartiall History of the Military Government of the Citie of Gloucester,* (Printed for R. Bostock, London, Pauls Church-yard, 1647), (E.402(4), pgs.27-34.
[3] *Exact and Full Relation of all the Proceedings between the Cavaliers and the Northamptonshire forces at*

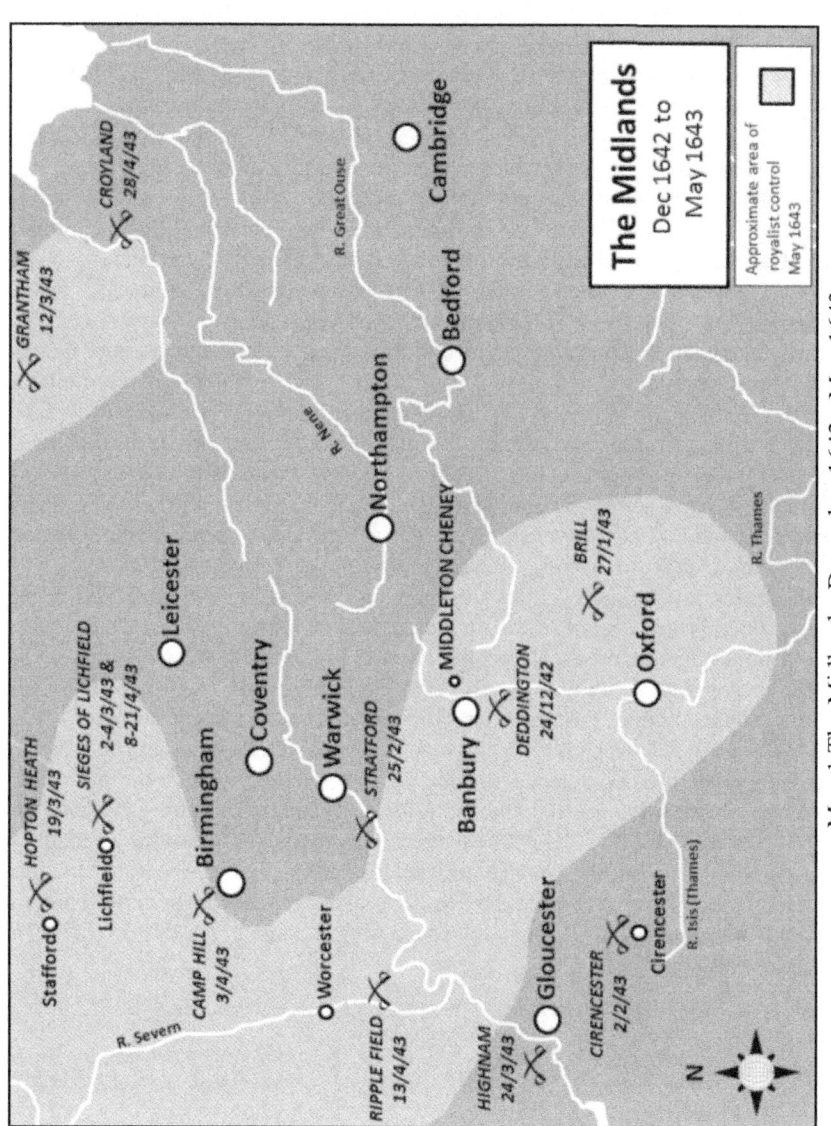

Map.1 The Midlands: December 1642 - May 1643 (**Map by the Author**)

Oxford, the Parliamentarians returned to threaten Banbury. Again, only the arrival of reinforcements prevented an attack on the town. Further south, the Parliamentarians attacked the outlying garrison at Brill on 27 January but were beaten off thanks, in part, to the Royalist's use of a smokescreen.[4] Lord Brooke, operating out of Warwick, was forced to eject a party of Royalists under Colonel Wagstaffe who had occupied Stratford. Events shifted to the north when Brooke took his small army to besiege Royalist-held Lichfield. The town capitulated after a short siege, but the Parliamentarians suffered a grievous loss when a sniper killed Lord Brooke.[5]

His successor, Sir John Gell, then moved towards Stafford. He was followed in March by the Earl of Northampton with orders to prevent the town's loss. Gell had summoned further reinforcements from the county under Sir William Brereton. The two commanders met at Hopton Heath but were engaged by the Earl and his small army. The battle was fierce as Northampton launched three successive cavalry charges against his opponents. The first charge successfully routed the Parliamentarian cavalry. The Earl led the second and, although it drove back Gell's infantry and captured his artillery, the Royalist commander was unhorsed and slain after 'he scorned to take quarter from such base rogues & Rebels'.[6] Sir Thomas Byron led the third charge, which almost routed the opposing infantry. Still, the Parliamentarians managed to hold their ground. Gell and Brereton soon withdrew off the battlefield and retired to their respective commands.[7] The Royalists' victory was somewhat pyrrhic. Although they managed to remove the threat to Stafford, this was offset by the loss of the Earl. His eldest son, James, now the 3rd Earl of Northampton, took command of the army and eventually joined Prince Rupert in his attempt to retake Lichfield.

Now in Parliamentarian hands, Lichfield would prove an obstacle to the Queen, who intended to march south with a small army. In early April, the Royalists began their attempt to recapture it. Prince Rupert was sent north with a strong army of horse and foot to clear a path for the Queen's army. Arriving outside Birmingham on 3 April, he immediately attacked and defeated the defending troops at the Battle of Camp Hill. The town was notoriously sacked by the victorious Royalists. Continuing northwards, the Prince reached Lichfield on 8 April. The Parliamentarian defenders were quickly chased out of the town, but the heavily fortified Cathedral Close was another matter. All attempts to take it were rebuffed, and Rupert's artillery was not powerful enough to breach the thick stout walls. Calling up miners from Cannock, the Prince ordered a tunnel dug beneath the wall.[8]

Banbury, (BL/TT/E.84(10). *The Perfect Diurnall,* (BLT/TT/E.244(32). Eliot Warburton, *Memoirs of Prince Rupert, and the cavaliers,* Vol.II (London, Richard Bentley, 1849). p.83

[4] Anonymous, *The Latest intelligence of Prince Ruperts proceeding in Northamption-Shire and also Colonell Goodwins at Brill : both exprest in two letters / from hands of good Quality.* (London, 1642), (BL/Wing/L563), pgs.5-6.

[5] Roy Sherwood, *The Civil War in the Midlands 1642-51,* (Stroud, Alan Sutton Publishing Ltd, 1992), p.32

[6] *The Battaile on Hopton Heath in Staffordshire Betweene His Majesties Forces under the Right Honourable the Earle of Northampton and those Rebels, March 19* (Oxford, H.Hall, 1643), (BL/TT/E.99(18), p.5.

[7] Lipscombe, p.86-7

While Rupert was occupied with the siege at Lichfield, the army commanded by the Earl of Essex advanced into Berkshire and laid siege to Reading. The garrison sent pleas for relief to Oxford, which obligated the King to recall most of his commanders and advance to save the town. Rupert, who the King also needed, was implored to bring his men south to assist in the relief. The Prince, holding his nerve, stacked the tunnel with barrels of powder and, on 20 April, detonated the first mine in the history of English warfare. A significant breach was made into which Rupert's troops surged, and the garrison, unable to hold out, surrendered on 21 April.[9] Rupert left Colonel Henry Hastings in command and marched to join the King at Reading. Detaching the new Earl of Northampton and the Prince of Wales' regiment to continue recruiting in the Banbury area, the Prince continued south to meet the King. The Earl of Northampton was also made responsible for ensuring that a munitions convoy, daily expected, would be safely conveyed to Oxford. Whilst awaiting this convoy, he would have to face a new Parliamentarian attack on Banbury.

Fig.2 A romanticised view of the 2nd Earl of Northampton just before his death at the Battle of Hopton Heath.
(Author's Collection)

---
[8] Royle, p.226
[9] Ibid, pp.226-27.

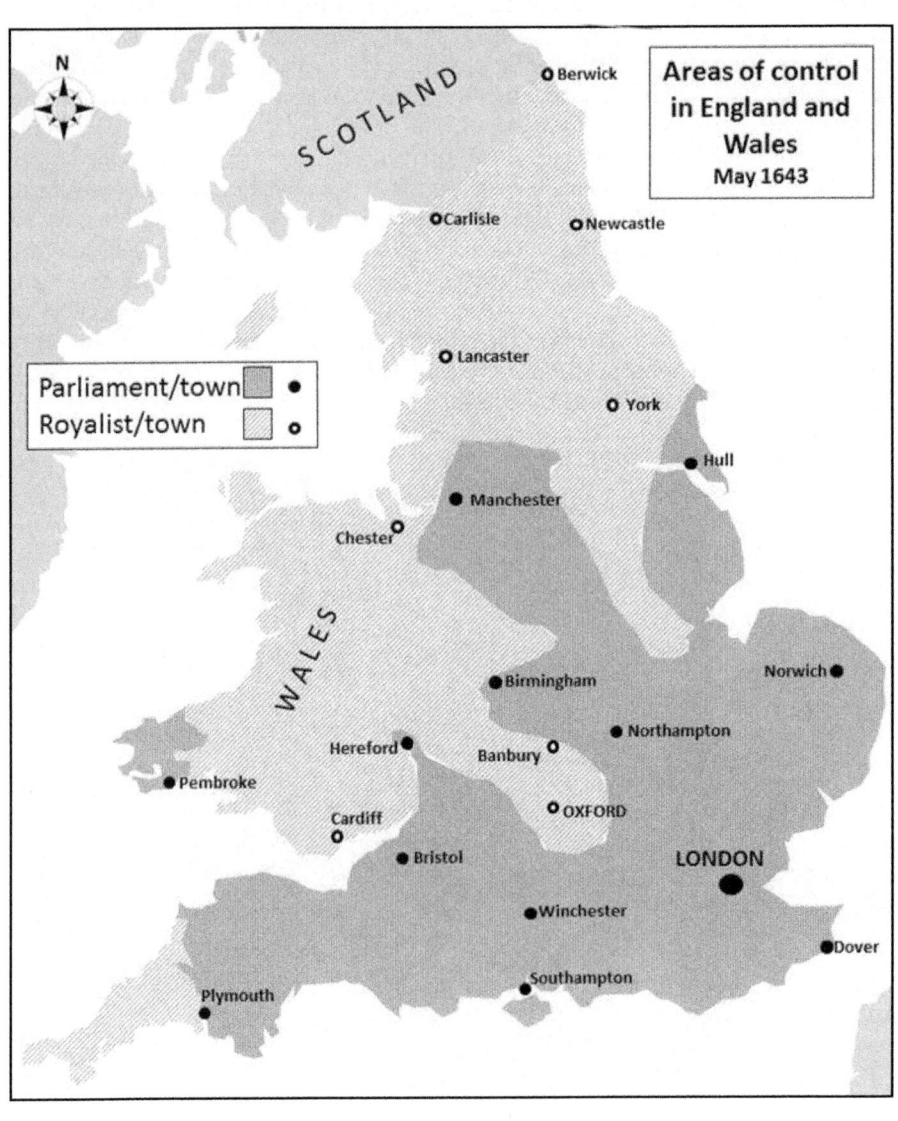

Map.2 Areas of control in England and Wales - May 1643
(Map by the Author)

Armies and weapons during the Civil War

Before we go on to discuss the forces available to each side during the campaign and the battle, this next section contains a brief description of the sorts of troops and equipment available to both sides during the conflict. It is included here for the benefit of those who have picked this publication up due to an interest in local history, rather than a fascination with the battles of the mid-17th century, and may not be familiar the organisation and equipment of armies in Western Europe during this period.

Infantry

The fundamental component of infantry (or 'foot') in Civil War armies was the regiment. Regiments often acted independently or could be grouped into brigades or a *'Tertia'* under a single commander's control, which would be combined to form armies.[1] The regiment was more of an administrative unit commanded by a Colonel or Lieutenant-Colonel who was authorised to raise it on behalf of his sponsor, be it King, Parliament or a local magnate. As well as recruiting the required number of men, the Colonel supplied them and issued arms and equipment. Payment of the men's wages was usually the King's or Parliament's responsibility. A foot regiment was deployed on the battlefield as a fighting 'battalion'. If the unit's strength was sufficient, it could deploy in two battalions. English armies were heavily influenced by Dutch practice because many Englishmen had served in the Dutch army during the Republic's war against Spain. But the wider war in Europe also influenced English military practice and by 1643 foot battalions probably deployed in ranks six deep with a body of pikes in the centre and sleeves of musketeers on each side of the pikes.

The musketeers of the front rank presented their weapons whilst the second rank made ready. Once the front rank had discharged their muskets, they made their way to the rear of their files to begin the loading process again. Once the second rank had discharged, they, too, made their way to the back of the file to re-load. Every rank repeated this process, known as countermarching, so that a continuous fire could be given against an opponent. At some point in 1643 foot soldiers on both sides began to adopt the practice seen in Swedish armies during the Thirty Years War which involved 'salvee' or volley fire. Rather than the standard countermarch, the first two ranks now fired and retired together. Later a third rank was added where the front rank knelt, the second stooped forward, and the third stood.[2] This tactic could be highly effective at close range, particularly when followed immediately by a charge by the whole body with pikes, swords and muskets used as clubs.

---

[1] Armies of the 17th century could be as small as a few thousand men and therefore had no brigade structure within the command. Most of these small armies contained independent regiments under a single commander who was in charge of the whole. The higher command structures such as a division did not exist in the 17th century and although the term *'corpus'* was used to denote a large body of men, the numbered Army Corps was a product of a much later time.

[2] Keith Roberts, *Pike and Shot Tactics 1590-1660,* (Oxford, Osprey Publishing, 2010), p.49.

Fig.3 An infantry block deployment from Robert Streeter's map of Naseby.
(Author's Collection)

On the battlefield, foot battalions were arranged in a checkerboard style. Those in the second line were opposite the gaps left in the front line into which they could move in support of the front line. This style of deployment also allowed broken infantry units a route to rout past the second line without disrupting it and then reform, if possible.

Cavalry

There were two types of cavalry (or 'horse') used during the Civil War, the cuirassier and the harquebusier.[3] The cuirassier was a fully armoured cavalryman who was expensive to maintain and equip, and had become increasingly less common in Europe from the 1630s onwards. Only one Parliamentarian regiment was equipped entirely as cuirassiers, and by late 1643 they too had been transformed into a harquebusier regiment, though some may have retained their cuirassier armour. There were other soldiers that also rode to battle called dragoons. These, however, were not cavalrymen but were mounted infantry who dismounted to fight and who could be rushed to a particular point on a battlefield to meet a specific threat. They also took up scouting, foraging and picket duty in most civil war armies. It is unlikely that any cuirassiers were present at Middleton Cheney, though individual Royalist troopers

---

[3] To this list may be added the 'lancer' who were more common in Scottish Armies and the 'carbine' whose name eventually became interchangeable with that of the dragoon.

may have been equipped with cuirassier armour. Only one pro-Parliamentarian source mentions dragoons present at the battle and lists them as a separate contingent from the horse and foot. If there were any present, then no information has come to light about their activities.[4]

Fig.4 Cavalry deployment from Robert Streeter's map of Naseby.
(Author's Collection)

By the 1640s, the standard cavalryman across Europe was the harquebusier. Equipped with a helmet, back and breastplate, a strong buff leather coat and boots, he carried a carbine, sword and usually a pair of pistols. Not all civil war cavalrymen, however, were able to be this fully equipped until later in the war. Harquebusiers fought mounted using their pistols and carbines. Traditionally cuirassiers were dominant on the battlefield and the harquebusiers were used in support roles. With the general decline of cuirassiers across Europe in the 1630s, the harquebusiers soon became the main component of an army's cavalry.[5] On the battlefield, commanders drew up the cavalry in ranks and files. Initially, the number of men in a file was eight, although later, this was reduced to six. Cavalry regiments could also increase their frontage by decreasing the number of men in each file. The Swedes, however, developed new tactics, partly due to their experiences in their wars against Poland. The King of Sweden, Gustavus Adolphus (1594-1632), ordered his men to charge the enemy formations with the front ranks using a single pistol as soon as they came into contact.[6] The trooper could use his remaining pistol in the melee. By forming their men three

---

[4] John Tincey, *Soldiers of the English Civil War (2) Cavalry,* (Oxford, Osprey Publishing Ltd, 1990), p.7-8.
[5] Lipscombe, p.33.
[6] To charge meant moving from a trot to a canter and did not employ the fully-fledged gallop so often beloved by filmmakers. It was, however, a shock tactic, and it certainly made the Royalist cavalry more aggressive in the early years of the war.

ranks deep, the Swedish cavalry presented a more extended frontage which could then envelope an enemy formation. At the battle of Edgehill, the Royalist cavalry, under Rupert's direction, drew up only three ranks deep in the Swedish style and appear to have continued this throughout the war.[7]

Fig.5 A contemporary illustration of a cavalry engagement.
(Rijksmusuem, RP-P-OB-23.151, Licence CC0 1.0)

In the early period of the war, the Parliamentarians mostly preferred to receive the Royalist charge from a stationary position with the front rank discharging their carbines at the enemy formation with the aim of disorganising and breaking-up the opposing formation before launching a counter-charge, although after several defeats, the Parliamentarians began to adopt Royalist tactics. The other difference between these two systems was command and control. Whilst the Royalists were undoubtedly more aggressive, they were generally unable to control their cavalry to enable a second charge. At Edgehill and Naseby, Rupert's cavalry streamed off the field in pursuit of their enemy, leaving their foot to fend for themselves. By 1645 the Parliamentarians had not only learned these tactics but were better able to control their men, with disastrous results for the Royalists.[8]

---

[7] John Tincey, *The Caracole: Is it Leading us Around in Circles?* In: Arquebusier : The Journal of the Pike and Shot Society, XXXVII/III, (Witney, Pike and Shot Society, 2020), p.20-37.
[8] Lipscombe, p.35.

Artillery

Artillery was becoming increasingly important in warfare, both for sieges and for field battles. Guns were not named, as now, by either the weight of shot or calibre of the barrel, but were given general names. These included names such as saker, falcon, robinet and drake. The artillery present at Middleton Cheney is referred to with the term 'drake'. Contemporary use of the term 'drake' usually signified a light field piece which fired a 3lb or 6lb shot. The drake had a shortened barrel and tapered breach, holding a smaller charge. This allowed the walls of the barrel to be thinner, significantly reducing its weight and making the ordnance more manoeuvrable.[9] In England, drakes were initially used in warships, being light enough not to overbalance the ship. A military manual of the day described them as being five feet long with a three-three-quarter inch bore and carrying a 6-pound weight of shot.[10] The term drake, however, seems to be a reference to the tapering breach chamber. The shortened barrel, however, made them less accurate, so they were mostly used as infantry support weapons for engaging the enemy at close range with case shot. The term 'drake' could also be used in conjunction with the names of other artillery types to denote a shorter and lighter variant of the gun in question with a tapered breach.[11] Without a detailed description, it is not always possible to be sure which type it is. The most common field guns were the 3lb Drake, the Saker and the Saker-drake. The shot weight of a Saker was approximately 6lbs. Based on its weight of shot, the Saker was one of the heavier field pieces.

Most Civil War armies carried drakes in their artillery trains, which were used extensively in the field. In 1642, the Earl of Essex's artillery train contained eleven drakes of 3lb bullet[12] whilst both artillery trains at the battle of Naseby in 1645 included Sakers the Parliamentarian train also included Saker-Drakes.[13] To move the ordnance on campaign teams of horses were used, though once deployed on the battlefield, 17th century artillery was not easy to move. For example, a Saker weighing approximately 1,500 - 1,900 lbs would require a team of five horses and at least seven men to move it on and off the battlefield.[14] Even the lighter guns, such as falcons and minions, were not easily manoeuvrable, especially over wet ground. The drakes, however, were light enough to be moved by one or two horses or a gun crew of three of four men. Usually, light field pieces were attached to individual regiments during battle, with heavier guns often grouped together to form a grand battery. A chest was also laid on the gun carriage with tools and a small supply of ammunition for speedy deployment.[15] Spare wagons

---

[9] Stephen Bull, *The Furie of the Ordnance; Artillery in the English Civil Wars*, (Woodbridge, The Boydell Press, 2008), p.12.

[10] Simon Marsh, *A Case of Drakes - James Wemyss and Artillery Innovations in the Civil Wars*, in: *A new way of fighting: Professionalism in the English Civil Wars*, (Solihull, Helion and Company Ltd, 2017), p.94

[11] David Blackmore, *Arms and Armour of the English Civil Wars*, (London, Royal Armouries, 1990), p.83.

[12] Simon Marsh, *The Train of Artillery of the Earl of Essex*, (Romford, The Pike & Shot Society, 2016), p.14.

[13] Blackmore, p.85.

[14] Lipscombe, p.33. The author includes a useful table of Artillery together with his sources.

Fig.6 A gun crew with their artillery piece.
(© **The Battlefields Trust**)

of ammunition and powder would be with the main train of guns. There is a reference at Middleton Cheney to at least one wagon accompanying the drake.[16]

The use of artillery on the battlefield was probably terrifying, especially if the other side were short of artillery and was also excellent for maintaining moral. The practice of the day was to fire iron balls that bounced along the ground and then ricocheted into the opposing ranks. Case shot, a long cylindrical tube made of wood or tin, could be particularly effective against packed ranks of infantry and also against cavalry. The tube contained a mass of musket balls. Once the ordnance was discharged, the tube split apart, sending a flying mass of musket shots into the opposing enemy formation. Whilst attempting to target a cavalryman at full canter with a single iron shot was almost impossible, the spread of case shot would undoubtedly be effective even against a moving target. However, once the opposing sides closed together and became intermixed, the artillery lost some of its effectiveness.

---

[15] Bull, pp.141-2.
[16] *Certaine Informations, Numb.17,* E.101(24).

The opposing armies - the Royalist brigade[1]

Before describing the battle we must take a look at the forces involved beginning with the Royalist brigade. James Compton, the 3rd Earl of Northampton, commanded the Royalists at Middleton Cheney. Born on 19 August 1622, the eldest of six brothers, the family were substantial landowners in both Warwickshire and Northamptonshire, and wielded considerable influence in both counties. Four of the other brothers fought alongside both their father and James during the war. On 20 March 1643, at the age of 21, James succeeded to the earldom following his father's death in battle. The young Earl was a brilliant commander of cavalry who often led a brigade of horse in the Oxford Army during the campaigns of 1643-45. He was also trusted with several independent commands during the War, which were conducted successfully. Despite these attributes, the Earl had an authoritarian personality which often led him to quarrel with his superiors, subordinates and family members, ultimately leading to him resigning his commission early in 1646.

In March of that year, he was given leave to come to the Committee for Compounding and compounded for his estates the following month[2]. The Earl played no part during the Second and Third Civil Wars, and after paying off his large fine in December 1651, he was allowed to enjoy the income from his estates.[3] The Earl was no stranger to the Commonwealth's prisons, spending short terms inside in 1651, 1653 and again in 1655 when Major-General William Boteler arrested him for unpaid taxes. He was also arrested on suspicion of complicity in the uprising of Sir George Booth in 1659, which led to his imprisonment in the Tower of London.[4] Following the Restoration, Charles II appointed him Lord Lieutenant of Warwickshire (1660-81) and Constable of the Tower (1675-79). He married twice and had two sons by his second marriage, including his heir, the fourth earl. Upon his death in 1681 at Castle Ashby, he was buried in the family church at Compton Wynyates.

All of the accounts note the presence of the Earl of Northampton's regiment at the battle of Middleton Cheney. James' father, Spencer Compton, the 2nd Earl of Northampton, was commissioned to form a unit of horse in the latter months of 1642. He began raising his regiment during the winter and spring of that year.[5] He made

---

[1] Whilst I have used the word brigade here, on this occasion it was more of an ad-hoc formation of two separate regiments with no formal structure.

[2] The Committee for Compounding with Delinquents was a Parliamentary body that enabled Royalists to recover their estates that had been confiscated during the war, by paying a fine. This process was known as 'compounding'.

[3] Hilton Kelliher, *A hitherto unrecognized cavalier dramatist: James Compton, third Earl of Northampton*, The British Library Journal, Vol. 6, No. 2 (AUTUMN 1980), p.163. *Calendar of the Proceedings of the Committee for Compounding, &c., 1643-1660: Cases, 1643-1646*, (Ed. Mary Anne Everett Green), (London, HMSO, 1890), p.1246-51

[4] Major-General Boteler to Mr Secretary Thurloe (Northampton - 13 November 1655). *A Collection of the State Papers of John Thurloe Esq; Vol. IV, Containing papers from September MDCLV to May MDCLVI*, (London, 1743), p.189. Kelliher, p.164.

Fig.7 James Compton, 3rd Earl of Northampton (1622-1681)
after William Dobson (London 1611?- London 1646)
CMS_PCF_129876 Collections - Public ©National Trust Images
(From an original painting in the Sackville Collection at Knole, Kent.
With the kind permission of Robert Sackville-West)

James the regiment's colonel, and another son, Charles, was appointed lieutenant-colonel. During the opening months of 1643, the regiment fought with Prince Rupert at Cirencester (2 February) and was at the battle of Hopton Heath (19 March) but was not complete when it was committed to action. James, when he succeeded to the Earldom, wrote to Prince Rupert that his father:

---

[5]BL Add. MSS 18980 f20 gives the commission date as 25 September. Sir Richard Bulstrode mentions that the date of the commission was after the Oxford Army retired to Winter quarters which was late in November/early December. Sir Richard Bulstrode, *Memoirs and Reflections upon the Reign and Government of King Charles the Ist and King Charles IId*. (London: Printed by N.Mist, for Charles Rivington, at the Bible and Crown in St. Pauls Churchyard, 1721), p.92-3). Peter Young, *The Prince of Wales Regiment of Horse 1642-1646*, (Leeds, Raider Books, 1988), p.5. Both give the date as 25 November 1642.

'had already raised three troops, besides his own, two of which were here present at the battle, the other was sent back from Henley in Arden to Banbury, for the security of that garrison.' [6]

Following Hopton Heath, the regiment did not immediately return to Banbury. A letter from Sir Edward Nicholas, the King's Secretary of State, to Prince Rupert noted that the Earl, in conjuncture with Colonel Henry Hastings, *'came to Belvoir Castle to recruit and refresh their troops'*.[7] Having been ordered to join Prince Rupert, Hastings attended the Prince at the siege of Lichfield (8-21 April). The move to Belvoir is confusing as the regiment was quartered at Henley in Arden throughout April. It was probably at Henley that James met Rupert on 31 March while the Prince rested on his way to Birmingham. Here the decision must have been made to send one troop back to Banbury. Accompanied by Hastings' regiment, the three remaining troops were sent further afield to rest after their efforts at Hopton Heath. Rupert eventually recalled them to assist him at Lichfield. Once Rupert had completed the siege, the Prince had to move quickly southwards to reunite his men with the rest of the Oxford Army, attempting to relieve the besieged troops in Reading.

As Rupert passed through Banbury on his return to Oxford, Northampton's regiment was detached to complete its recruitment and monitor any local Parliamentarian activity. Another concern was a munitions convoy expected from the north of England, which Northampton was to escort into Oxford from Banbury. Queen Henrietta Maria, having landed in Yorkshire in February 1643, had detached from York a convoy around the start of May with a large quantity of arms and ammunition destined for Oxford. The convoy was escorted to Newark by Sir Charles Cavendish, who would then pass responsibility to Henry Hastings. Hastings was to accompany the convoy to Banbury from Newark into the Earl of Northampton's charge for the safe delivery to Oxford. One of the Earl's responsibilities would have been to ensure that the local Parliamentarians did not intercept it. The convoy eventually arrived safely at Banbury and was conveyed to Woodstock near Oxford, where it arrived on 13 May.[8]

According to the sources, Northampton had between ten and thirteen troops under his command at Middleton Cheney. At this stage in the war, most regiments contained around six troops of horse, with each troop containing approximately 70 officers and men within its ranks. Initially, the Royalists called for regiments of 500 volunteers, which often meant that the troops were not evenly split. Some could even contain a greater number of troops than the regular size.[9] Northampton's regiment never

---

[6] Warburton, p.84.
[7] Warburton, p.160.
[8] *Mercurius Aulicus, The nineteenth Weeke*, Vol.1, p.259. Tennant, *Edgehill and Beyond*, p.111.
[9] John Tincey, *Soldiers of the English Civil War (2) Cavalry*, p.5-7. Peter Young, *The Cavalier Army; Its organisation and everyday life*, (Chatham, George Allen & Unwin Ltd, 1974), p.25-6.

contained as many as thirteen troops. By April 1644, a year after Middleton Cheney, it barely had 250 officers and men in its ranks.[10]

There must, therefore, have been more than one Royalist cavalry regiment present at the battle. By May 1643, there were two Royalist horse regiments in the Banbury area. The first, commanded by Colonel Gerard Croker of Hook Norton in Oxfordshire, was to the west of Banbury at the time of the battle. There were tensions between the Earl and Croker, and neither got on well with the other. The exasperated Earl wrote to Prince Rupert on 8 May complaining of Croker's conduct in his attempts *'to plunder Braiks [Brailes] and some other towns thereabouts'*.[11] The Earl also requested protection for Brailes *'and for the town of Long-Compton, which is mine'*.[12] There are no references to the Earl calling on Croker's regiment to assist him. It was probably too busy attempting to plunder Northampton's tenants at the time of the battle.

A more likely candidate for the other regiment is the Prince of Wales' Regiment of Horse. Initially raised in Yorkshire in 1642, the regiment originally contained seven troops commanded by peers and gentlemen, many of whom would later command their own regiments.[13] The regiment was commanded by Sir Thomas Byron of the famous Byron's of Newstead Abbey, who fought at Edgehill and was present at Turnham Green. The Oxford Army's dispersal into winter quarters on 9 December 1642 saw the regiment sent to Banbury accompanied by the Earl of Northampton's and Colonel John Belasyse's foot regiments.[14] During the opening months of 1643, it fought with Northampton's regiment at Cirencester and Hopton Heath. Sir Thomas sustained a wound in the thigh at Hopton Heath, which temporarily removed him from command. Byron's absence may account for Northampton's ability to divide the regiment between the senior officers at Middleton Cheney. Interestingly there is no mention of Sir Arnold de Lille, a Lieutenant Colonel who later commanded the regiment during Byron's absence.

Confirmation of the regiment's involvement can be obtained by examining those officers who were present at the action at Middleton Cheney. The senior officer involved was Major Thomas Daniel (post-1617-c.1682) of Beswick. Thomas was the third son born to Sir Ingelby Daniel and Frances Metham. He was knighted after the Restoration in 1662 and held the post of High Sheriff of Yorkshire in 1679. Daniel died in 1682 and was buried in London.[15] Major Daniel's association with the Prince of Wales' Regiment of Horse began in 1642 when he was a lieutenant in the Colonel's troop.[16] His promotion to Major (sometimes styled Sergeant-Major) appears rapid as

---

[10] Morris, Robert *The Battle of Cropredy Bridge 1644,* (Bristol, Stuart Press, 1994), p.14, 18.

[11] Most probably Upper Brailes, Lower Brailes or Sutton-under-Brailes which are 9 miles from Banbury and 4 miles from Long Compton.

[12] Warburton, pp.187-88.

[13] One example being the Earl of Northampton's troop.

[14] *BL Harleian MS 6851. f.237.* The Earl of Northampton's regiment quartered at Banbury was the foot regiment that later served as the permanent garrison of the castle.

[15] Stephen Leslie, (Ed.), *Dictionary of National Biography, Volume XIV, Damon-D'Eyncourt,* (London, Smith, Elder, & Co, 1888), p.21.

this was the rank he held at Middleton Cheney, even though the regiment was not mentioned by name as being present. He also commanded it at the Battle of Chalgrove Field (18 June 1643). The list of those regiments present at that engagement provides proof of this:

> 'His strength was near 2000 men: whereof about 1000. Horse under 3. Regiments. Those namely, of his Highness the Prince of Wales, commanded by Sergeant-Major Daniel.. "[17]

The author of the *Late Beating Up* recognised his courage in his account of the fighting at Chalgrove:

> 'The same mischance (and some slight wounds) had Sergeant-Major Daniel, by the fall of his Horse but being re-mounted, he in pursuit required it upon his adversaries, he having before that shot dead a Cornet of the Rebels, recovered the honour to the Prince.'[18]

A seemingly courageous and experienced officer, Daniel was placed in command of the right wing of Northampton's horse.

The other senior officer known to be present was Captain James Trist (d31 May 1644)[19], although there is little information on his life before the events of the Civil War. It may be the same Captain Trist who commanded the King's Guards during the Second Bishops' War and raised a petition against two troopers under his control for threatening the life of the Lord General, for challenging him to a duel and then later attempting to kill him.[20] Trist certainly belonged to the regiment by March 1644 when *Mercurius Aulicus*, relating the details of a skirmish at Adderbury, noted *'that expert Captaine Trist (of Prince CHARLES his Regiment)'*.[21] Before the events of May, Trist was captured and wounded in a skirmish at Stratford-upon-Avon. Being sorely hurt, Trist was left at Stratford but was promptly rescued by soldiers of the garrison at

---

[16] Young, *The Prince of Wales Regiment*, p.1.

[17] *His highnesse prince Ruperts late beating up the rebels quarters at Post-comb & Chinner in Oxfordshire. Also his victory in Chalgrove Field. Whereunto is added sr. Iohn Urries expedition to West-Wickham*. (Oxford, Leon Lichfield, 1643), Bodleian Library. Transcript at: https://johnhampdensregiment.org.uk/LateBeatingUp/#p=1 [Accessed: 7 October 2020], p.2.

[18] Ibid, p.9

[19] Trist's death was recorded by Sir Edward Walker in his entry for the 30-31 May 1644 during the attack on Abingdon to cover the King's withdrawal during the second siege of Oxford. Walker writes of 'the loss of Captain de Lyne of Prince Charles Regiment, and Captain Trist, and some few more wounded.' Sir Edward Walker, *Historical Discourses upon Several Occasions*, (Ed. by H. Clapton), (London: Printed for Samuel Keble, 1705), p.17.

[20] *Journal of the House of Lords, Volume IV, Charles I, 1625-1642*, (No date or publisher), p.425.

[21] *Mercurius Aulicus; Communicating the Intelligence and affaires of the Court, to the rest of the kingdome'*, in: *The English Revolution III, Newsbooks I, Oxford Royalist, Volume 3*. Ed. by Robin Jeffs, et al., (London: Cornmarket Press, 1971), p.417.

Banbury. Seeking to waylay Trist on his return, Mistress Elizabeth Phillips, wife to the local magistrate of Banbury, sent a message with a certain William Needle to the Parliamentarian troops quartered at Bicester. Their object was to intercept the Banbury party on their return to the town. Unfortunately, Needle was apprehended by members of the Banbury garrison. Forced to confess his mission, Colonel Henry Hunks hanged him in the marketplace while Mistress Phillips was imprisoned.[22] Trist recovered in time to join the action at Middleton Cheney, where he proved his skill as a cavalry commander. Daniel's and Trist's association with the Prince of Wales' regiment suggests it was the regiment that was with Northampton's at Middleton Cheney.

Only the Royalist *Mercurius Aulicus* and a letter written by Philip Willoughby to Prince Rupert (see table 1, p33) provide the strength of the Royalist brigade at the battle. These two sources mention that there were between ten and thirteen troops of horse present. One of the original seven troops from the Prince of Wales' Regiment was detached under the Earl of Northampton to provide a nucleus for his newly commissioned regiment. The evidence of the letter sent to Prince Rupert indicates that in March 1643, the Earl's regiment had at least four troops of horse. Unfortunately, there is no evidence of whether Northampton had successfully raised any more troops by early May or whether the one detached to Banbury was successful with its recruiting. The Prince of Wales' Regiment initially contained seven troops and likely still had six whilst at Banbury. It therefore seems likely that the lowest estimate of ten troops is the most probable. Both regiments had been continuously fighting since February. Allowing for the usual wastage in men killed, sick or deserted, Northampton may have had between 500-600 men available to fight in the upcoming battle. Three days previously, during the fire at Banbury, it was reported that there were 400 soldiers in the town, but this may only be a reference to the foot regiment garrisoning the castle.[23] Unfortunately, the information contained in the sources is too scant to propose an exact figure for the Royalist force that fought at Middleton Cheney.

---

[22] *A Perfect Relation of the Cause and Manner of the Apprehending, by the Kings Souldiers, William Needle and Mistris Phillips*, (BL/TT/E.247(13), 1643.

[23] *A Continuation of Certaine Special and remarkable Passages*, Num.44, (Cooke & Wood) (BL/TT/E.249(4), London, 1643. There would be little space within the town itself to accommodate two further regiments. The horse were probably quartered in the surrounding villages.

The opposing armies - Parliament's force from Northampton

Whilst there is enough information to gauge the composition of the Royalist forces, that of the Parliamentarians is less well documented. No account or letter has survived from anyone who fought on the Parliamentarian side. Most of the information available stems from the newspapers and pamphlets written and issued in London and so have the problems of reliability outlined in the introduction.[1]

The one detail consistent with all available sources is that the Parliamentarian force came, for the most part, from the town of Northampton. There are frequent references to the 'Northamptonshire Forces'[2] and other references to the town itself. Alas, none of the sources clearly state who was in overall command and who they were commanding. That there was an overall commander is certain as more than one newspaper refers to 'he that commanded in chiefe.'[3] Only two accounts mention the identity of this unknown commander. The chronicle of James Heath, published in 1675, identified Colonel John Fiennes as the commander of the combined force.[4] However, the identification of this officer can be shown to be incorrect. During May 1643, 'Colonel' Fiennes was only a captain and commanded a troop in his elder brother's regiment at Bristol. Heath may have used the last rank he obtained when he was commissioned to raise a regiment of horse in 1644. The other source is *Speciall Passages, number 40*. Unfortunately, the edition containing the details of the battle is now missing. Alfred Beesley's *'The History of Banbury'* preserves only a summary, but importantly it says that:

'...the whole commanded by the sergeant-major of Colonel Barkley.'[5]

---

[1] The same can equally be said of Royalist newspapers. *Mercurius Aulicus* was written and printed at Oxford during the war from 1643-45. *Mercurius Aulicus* and some of its Parliamentarian counterparts such as *Mercurius Civicus*, *Mercurius Britannicus* and *The Scottish Dove* often spent much of their time refuting each other's news.

[2] *Mercurius Civicus, Number 1, 4th-11th May 1643*. Volume I, 4th May - 28th December 1643. Ed. Jones, S.F. (Tygers Head Books, 2013), p.12.

[3] *A Perfect Diurnall of the Passages in Parliament, Numb.48,* (Coles & Leach), (BL/TT/E.249(6). *Speciall Passages, No.40*. Brief summery in Beesley, "The History of Banbury", fn.32. p.377.

[4] James Heath, *A Chronicle of the Late Intestine War in the Three Kingdoms of England, Scotland and Ireland, With the Intervening Affairs of Treaties, and Other Occurrences Relating Thereunto. As Also the Several Usurpations, Forreign Wars, Differences and Interests Depending Upon It, to the Happy Restitution of Our Sacred Soveraign K. Charles II. In Four Parts, Viz. The Commons War, Democracie, Protectorate, Restitution* (Printed by J.E, for Thomas Basset, at the George, Cliffords-Inn in Fleetstreet, London, 1676), p.46.

[5] Alfred Beesley, *The History of Banbury: Including Copious Historical and Antiquarian Notices of the Neighborhood* (London, Nichols and Son, 1841) fn32, p.347. Alas, issue number 40 is missing from the volumes currently in the British Library. It was certainly available to Alfred Beesley who provides a very brief summary of some of the details in his book. Unfortunately he does not quote directly from the source.

Whilst there were many officers with variations of this surname, the correct identification is probably that of Colonel David Berkley, whose regiment of foot was in garrison at Northampton in 1643.[6] An entry in the accounts for Northampton twelve days after the battle appears to confirm this:

'*18 May 1643*
___ to appoint you to pay unto Colonell Ba___ ___forwards ___ arrears of the pay of Captaine Melvill fifty ___ ___ pounds.'[7]

Unfortunately, only the first two letters of the Colonel's surname are preserved in the document, but he reappears again some months later in August with his surname in full:

'*15 August 1643*
___ leave to appoint you to pay unto Collonell Barclay in ___ of payment of the money due to him for his owing pay ___ the some of fiftie poundes out of _ur_ money as is in yor fundes, and for so doing this shall bee yor warrant.
Richard Samwell
Ed. Hasby'[8]

Despite the fragmentary nature of the sources, it is clear that the 'Collonell Barclay', who appears in May, is the same person mentioned in August. Furthermore, this conforms to the fragment of the *Speciall Passages* cited by Beesley in his account of the battle. This leads us to conclude that it was indeed Colonel David Berkley's regiment, or part of it at least, which fought at Middleton Cheney.

Information on the exact composition of this regiment is scarce. It had disappeared by September 1643, perhaps due to losses at Middleton Cheney. More likely it was probably disbanded and merged into the foot regiment raised in September by the governor of Northampton, Nathaniel Whetham.[9] The strength of the unit is not consistent between the different accounts. Both Royalist sources gave an identical strength of 6-700 foot, although it is probable that the newspaper *Mercurius Aulicus* used the figures from Philip Willoughby's letter to Prince Rupert of the 7 May.[10] 17th century newspapers frequently exaggerated the opposing numbers to enhance the nature of any victory or to downplay any defeat in the eyes of their readers. Because of this, there is a wide range of figures between the different sources. The lowest estimate given is that there were 300 foot present at the battle.[11] Other sources provide

---
[6] BCW Regimental Page, Parliamentarian, Foot Regiments. http://wiki.bcw-project.org/Parliamentarian/foot-regiments/col.-david-berkley [accessed 4/10/21]. Unfortunately this entry is unsourced.
[7] The National Archives (TNA), SP28/238 v.4 f.640.
[8] TNA, SP28/238 v.4 f.686.
[9] Whetham was appointed Governor in March 1643.
[10] Warburton, Vol.II, p.186. *Mercurius Aulicus,* Vol.I, p.256
[11] *Speciall Passages, No.40.* Beesley, fn.32. p.377.

a closer degree of numbers, with *Mercurius Civicus* stating that there was 500 foot present.[12] Two other newspapers present a figure of 500, but here both the horse and foot are combined into one total.[13] If the troops of horse at Middleton Cheney contained approximately 200 men, then the figure of 500 foot would conform to the summary in *Speciall Passages*.[14] However, as this newspaper is missing, there is no way to be sure. *Mercurius Civicus* does not list any horse and may have grouped these figures together. Nonetheless, the Royalist account from *Mercurius Aulicus* indicated 566 infantry weapons were captured from the Parliamentarians after the battle (see below), suggesting that the 500 figure represented only the foot and that this may have been an underestimate.

The captains of the Northampton garrison are listed in the accounts. Captains Lawson, Gifford, Melville, Martin, Symfroy, Woodford, Pentlowe and Sawyer are mentioned in the months before the battle on 6 May.[15] Martin is mentioned by name in the Royalist newspaper *Mercurius Aulicus* and was in command of a company of foot in the Northampton garrison. Two more officers, Lieutenant Cotton (associated with Captain Melville) and Lieutenant Glover with Captain Martin, appear in the accounts, though whether they fought in the battle is unknown.[16] Based on the incomplete evidence, the most we can produce is a small list of officers present in the Northampton garrison between February and May 1643. There is no evidence that any of these men, except Captain Martin, were present at the battle.

We have no information on the deployments used at Middleton Cheney besides the Parliamentarians being able to shoot their muskets at the Earl's cavalrymen. On this occasion, the Northamptonshire force had a larger ratio of musketeers to pikemen than was considered desirable. If the account in *Mercurius Aulicus* is to be believed, the Royalists captured 416 muskets and 150 pikes. If correct, this would give a musket-to-pike ratio of 2.8:1 for the battle. This shortfall in pike protection for the musketeers gave the Earl's cavalry an advantage.

The accounts are even more confused when mentioning the Parliamentarian cavalry. There is no reference to a regimental structure, and independent troops of horse are listed under many different captains. Only the Royalist sources give the specific number of troops that served on the Parliamentarian side, whilst only the fragmentary summary of *Speciall Passages* notes any figures. The sources agree that there were between three and four Parliamentarian troops of horse present. There were also four different names mentioned for the commanding officers. The list is not without problems, as at least one of these officers may not have even been present. The first to be named was Captain Sawyer. Sawyer (or Sayer) may have been the man

---

[12] *Mercurius Civicus, Number 1*. p.12
[13] *Certaine Informations from severall parts of the Kingdome, Num.17*, (BL/TT/E.101(4), London, 1643. *A Perfect Diurnall, Numb.49*. Tuesday 9th May.
[14] *Speciall Passages, No.40*. Beesley, fn.32. p.377.
[15] Respectively TNA, SP28/238; v.1 f.59 / v.2 f.569 / v.4 f.591, 596, 599, 601, 602 & 603.
[16] TNA, SP28/238 v.4 f.627,633.

listed as a cornet in Asycough's troop of horse in the Earl of Essex's Army in the summer of 1642.[17] A more probable identification would be that of Captain Francis Sawyer, known to have served in Northampton in November 1642.[18] Two London newspapers note his involvement at Middleton Cheney, namely the *Continuation* and the *Perfect Diurnall*. The *Perfect Diurnall* speaks of:

'500. horse and Dragoones, and some Foot under the command of Captain Martin, Captain Needham, and Captain Sawyer...' [19]

The description of the battle in the Continuation adds further details:

'Captaine Sawyer was quartered at Clayden about 6 or 8 miles beyond Ailsbury, some of his scouts were taken by the Kings forces, and the said Captaine Sayer and Captaine Martine marched forth with their Troops (being Bedfordshire men) thinking to rescue their scouts, 3 or 4 Troops of the Kings forces which came from Banbury or thereabouts...' [20]

The problem with Sawyer's presence at Middleton Cheney is mainly due to a conflicting account in the Royalist newspaper *Mercurius Aulicus*. According to the report, Sawyer was killed in a skirmish at Bicester on the same day as Middleton Cheney. It is worth repeating this account in full below to gain an idea of the similarities between the two engagements:

'This day, a party of 40 Horse of Sir John Byrons Regiment, scouting about the Country towards Bisester (a Towne about 12 miles from Oxford) met with a party of 200 Horse of the Rebels Army; and charged so valiantly upon them, that notwithstanding the great oddes in number (being five for one) they killed 25 of them in the skirmish, whereof Captaine Sawyer was one, tooke 12 prisoners, and put all the rest to a shamefull flight; not one of the Kings soldiers being killed or hurt.' [21]

Of the fight, Parliamentarian accounts state that:

---

[17] 'Surnames beginning 'S", in The Cromwell Association Online Directory of Parliamentarian Army Officers, ed. Stephen K Roberts (2017), British History Online http://www.british-history.ac.uk/no-series/cromwell-army-officers/surnames-s [accessed 20 October 2020].
[18] TNA, SP28/262 f.186, December 1642. It is possible however that this Sawyer is the man referred to as being killed in a skirmish at Wellingborough in December 1642 in a letter from the Earl of Northampton to Prince Rupert. Warburton, Memoirs of Prince Rupert, Vol.II, p.84. (Earl of Northampton, to Prince Rupert, Banbury, 27 December 1642)
[19] *A Perfect Diurnall, Numb.49*. Tuesday 9th May.
[20] *A Continuation of Certaine Speciall and Remarkable Passages, Thursday the 4. of May. till Thursday the 11. of the same, 1643*, (BL/TT/E.249(4)
[21] *Mercurius Aulicus; The Eighteenth Weeke*. Vol 1. p.256.

'there was a great fight between the Kings forces that were about Banbury, and the Parliaments, some of them being quartered at Northampton, and others of them in the lower part of Buckinghamshire, the Parliament's forces consisting of about 500 horse and Dragoones, and some Foot, under the command of Captain Martin, Captain Needham, and Captain Sawyer... [the Royalists] fell upon the Parliaments Forces suddenly, slew about 50 and took 300 prisoners, and it was thought Captain Sawyer was killed...' [22]

Intelligence received by the Earl of Essex's Scoutmaster, Sir Samuel Luke, on 7 May 1643 also reported a skirmish at Claydon in which 'Captain Sayers' was slain.[23] Given this and notwithstanding the apparent bias and triumphant tone of *Mercurius Aulicus*, it seems likely that there were two separate skirmishes. When reading the Parliamentarian sources some have mixed both encounters into a single engagement, but it appears that Sawyer was killed at either Bicester or Claydon and, therefore, was not present at Middleton Cheney. A possible explanation is that Sawyer and the other troops may have originally intended to join the Northamptonshire forces about Banbury. Unfortunately, Sawyer became entangled with Byron's detachment leaving the other cavalry troops to press on to Banbury alone.

The second officer, Captain Martin, is present in both Royalist and Parliamentarian accounts. Here once again, there is confusion. As discussed above, a Captain Martin was undoubtedly present in the Northampton garrison commanding a company of foot. Another report has him associated with both Sawyer and Needham, and another places him at Bicester.[24] Martin and Sawyer's troops also contained 'Bedfordshire men' according to one account.[25] The association in the accounts with the cavalry begs the question, was there more than one Captain Martin present at the battle? Or is the simplest explanation that Martin, being a prominent officer named as captured, was inserted into the accounts without the author having specific knowledge of who he was or from where he originated?

The third Captain present was called Needham. Only the *Perfect Diurnall* mentions him, and information is scarce concerning this officer. The final officer noted, Captain Melvin, only appears in the Royalist accounts, with *Mercurius Aulicus* calling him a 'Scottish man'.[26] The officer in question may have been Captain David Melvin, who commanded a troop of harquebusiers in the army of the Earl of Essex and who later fought at the first battle of Newbury (September 1643). By 1644 he was a major and a reformado[27] of horse and was still active at the end of the First Civil War.[28] In 1648

---

[22] *A Perfect Diurnall, Numb.49. Tuesday 9th May*

[23] I.G.Philip. *Journal of Sir Samuel Luke,* (Banbury: Cheney & Sons, 1950), p.71

[24] *Mercurius Aulicus, The Eighteenth Weeke, Vol 1,* p.257. *A Perfect Diurnall, Numb.49. Tuesday 9th May. A Continuation of Certaine Special and remarkable Passages, Num.44.*

[25] *A Continuation of Certaine Speciall and Remarkable Passages from both Houses of Parliament, and other Parts of the Kingdom. From Thursday the 4. of May. till Thursday the 11. of the same, 1643,* (Cooke & Wood) (BL/TT/E.249(4)

[26] *Mercurius Aulicus, The Eighteenth Weeke , Vol 1,* p.257.

Melvin petitioned Parliament for damages owed whilst at Tickhill in 1646. The locals, furious at Scottish quartering, attacked and wounded the officer before stripping him of his clothes and robbing him.[29] The date of his death is unknown, but in 1673 a will was entered by David Melvin of Leven in Fifeshire which may also be the former officer.[30] It is also possible that *Mercurius Aulicus* misprinted his name from Melville to Melvin. Captain Melville commanded a company of foot in the Northampton garrison and was more likely to have been taken prisoner than a cavalry officer. Melville's origins, however, are unknown. Looking at the different accounts, it is clear that there were at least three Captains of horse present at Middleton Cheney. Although this accords with at least some of the known accounts, without further detailed evidence, we cannot make a definite determination. If all of the horse troops were at full strength, then, including officers, there would be around 210 men in total. The correct figure will surely be lower, and only the incomplete summary of the *Speciall Passages* gives specific numbers engaged on the Parliamentary side.

As with the infantry there is little evidence of the tactics used by either side in the battle at Middleton Cheney, although there is at least one reference to Northampton being able to control his troops and return them rapidly to action. Nevertheless, it is likely that the Royalist cavalry deployed and fought in the way they had at Edgehill given that Northampton had been present at that battle and that the Parliamentarian horse followed the early war practice of receiving the charge at the standstill whilst firing carbines.

All but two of the accounts agree on the presence of artillery at the battle. Two versions name the guns employed as a 'Drake' whilst only in a letter is any measurement given when Philip Willoughby described the capture of *'one piece of cannon of six-pound bullet'* said to be made of brass.[31]

At Middleton Cheney, apart from the description of the ordnance used by the Parliamentarians as a drake, there is no further information about its employment during the battle or location on the battlefield. Without further detail, we must take Philip Willoughby's description to determine that the ordnance employed at Middleton Cheney was most likely a Saker-drake with a shot weight of 6lb. The Parliamentarians claimed that the drake caused the majority of the casualties during the battle.[32] If this is to be believed, then it was not entirely ineffective, even against an enemy force wholly composed of cavalry.

---

[27] A reformado was an officer who still held his rank, despite his unit having been disbanded or amalgamated.
[28] TNA SP28/10 ff.259-60 and SP28/18 f.31.
[29] *'House of Lords Journal Volume 9: 1 May 1647'*, in Journal of the House of Lords: Volume 9, 1646 (London, 1767-1830), pp. 165-173. British History Online http://www.british-history.ac.uk/lords-jrnl/vol9/pp165-173 [accessed 21 October 2020]. HL/PO/JO/10/1/265, 25/7/1648. Robert Ashton, *Counter Revolution, The Second Civil War and its Origins, 1646-8,* (Avon, The Bath Press, 1994), p.308-9.
[30] TNA, PROB 11/342/687.
[31] Warburton, Vol.II, p.186.
[32] *A Perfect Diurnall Numb.48.*

Table 1		
Royalist and Parliamentarian strengths at Middleton Cheney		
Source	**Parliamentarian**	**Royalist**
Mercurius Aulicus (R)	700 foot 3-4 troops of horse 1 cannon	10-12 troops of horse
Philip Willoughby (R)	6-700 foot 4 troops of horse 1 cannon	13 troops of horse
Certain Informations, 17 (P)	500 horse and foot 1 drake	
A Perfect Diurnall, 49 (P)	500 horse and dragoons Few foot	
Speciall Passages (P)	300 foot 120 horse (3 troops)	
A Perfect Diurnall, 48 (P)	600 1 drake	
Mercurius Civicus, 1 (P)	500 foot	
Continuation (Coles & Leach) (P)	600 1 drake	

Banbury and Middleton Cheney in 1643

In 1643 Banbury was a small market town of approximately 1600 people. The heart of the town was based around the market square and boasted at least two mills, a gaol, a former hospital, a manor for the former abbot and the Church of St. Mary. A ditch ran around the town, and there were four gates or 'bars' to control traffic and levy tolls. The most prominent building, however, and one which dominated the town, was the castle. Originally a bishop's palace built during the reign of King Henry I by Alexander, Bishop of Lincoln, it was expanded extensively during the reign of Henry III into a concentric castle with double gateways and moats. Before the war, the Fiennes family, who were the local magnates, leased the castle. Banbury's leading trade was in shoes and wool, and James I had made Banbury a mayoral town with the issue of a charter in 1608, which had also granted Banbury a wool market.[1] Although a flourishing market town, a great fire in 1628 burned down many of the houses, and the Civil War would add further misfortune. The practising religion of the inhabitants at the beginning of the 17th Century had become distinctly Puritan. Two crosses in Banbury were destroyed on 26 July 1600 in an outbreak of iconoclasm while many of its vicars preached Puritan ideas.[2] William Fiennes, 1st Viscount Saye and Sele and the senior north Oxfordshire magnate was also Puritan. The family seat was at Broughton Castle, three miles southwest of the town. While the father sat in the House of Lords, his eldest son James was returned as MP for Banbury in 1625. The second son Nathaniel was returned for the town in the Long Parliament in 1640. Whilst the Fiennes family dominated local politics around Banbury and northern Oxfordshire, their rivals, the Compton Earls of Northampton, did the same for southern Warwickshire. The Compton family seat was at Compton Wynyates, only seven miles distant.

Banbury castle would eventually become a strong Royalist garrison. Under Parliamentarian control before the battle of Edgehill, the castle and town were captured by the Royalists on 27 October 1642. Once the King had established his capital at Oxford in December 1642, the town stood at the northern apex of a series of garrisons that were supposed to help protect it.[3] Despite its small size, Banbury was a strong garrison and an essential trading centre for the Royalists. In 1644 Colonel Whetham penned a letter describing the then-current siege but also of Banbury's importance to Oxford:

'The Castle is of more concernement to Oxford than any other, for besides the provisions of victuals by droves of Sheep and Beasts weekely, it is upon good ground aver'd that for a long time this garrison hath payd 18000 per weeke to Oxford, divers

---
[1] Beesley, 254-58.
[2] Ibid, p.244-45
[3] The system of garrisons designed to protect Oxford was not a continuous defensive circuit. Local Parliamentarian forces and also larger armies were frequently able to penetrate through the gaps right up to Oxford itself.

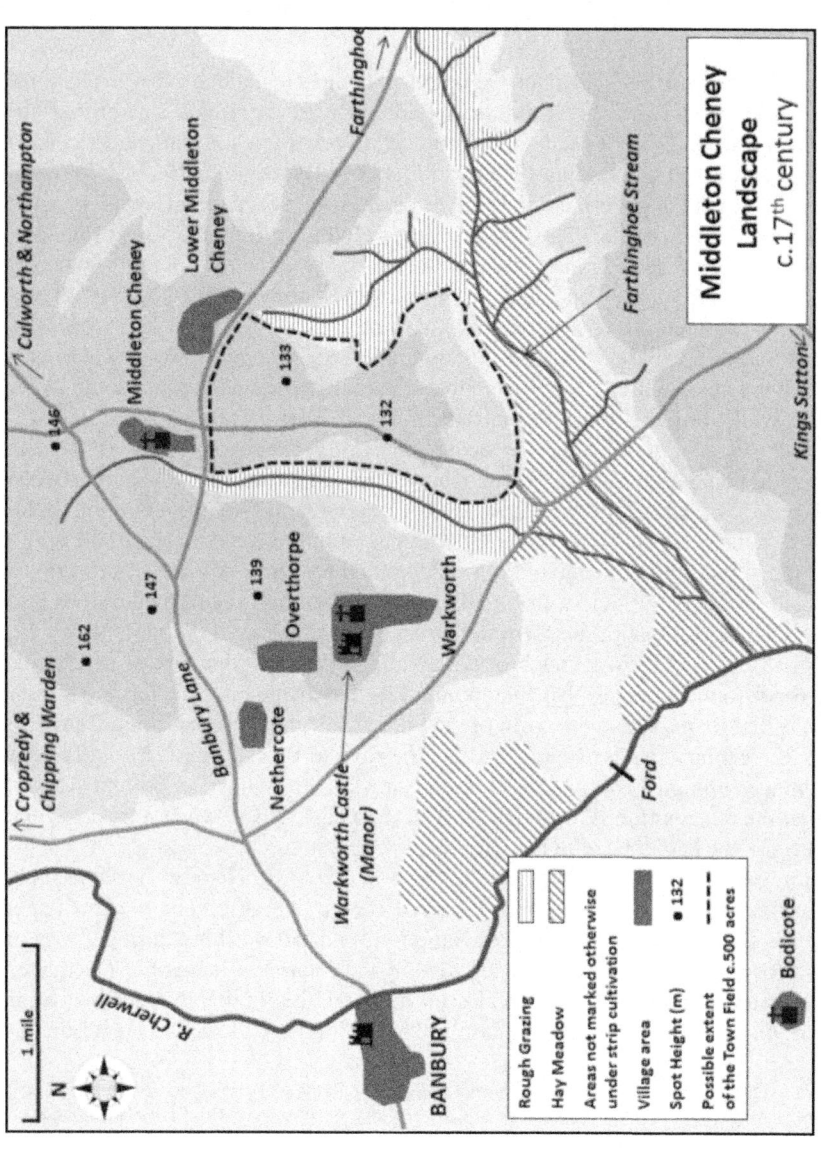

Map.3 Middleton Cheney and Warkworth Parishes (c.1643)
(Computerised map from a hand-drawn original by Deborah Hayter)

towns being taxed to more than the yeerley revenue of them; so that the taking...would much conduce to the straitning of Oxen [Oxford], and give liberty of Trade to London from Many parts.' [4]

Control of the town also aided the Compton's attempts to maintain Royalist control of southern Warwickshire. Their tenure at Banbury was very much a family affair. Following the second Earl's death at Hopton Heath, his eldest son, James, succeeded to his titles and offices, including the governorship of Banbury. In 1644 Sir William Compton took over the governorship from his elder brother James. They were assisted by professional soldiers such as Colonel Henry Hunks and later Colonel Anthony Greene and when not serving in the field with the horse regiment, another brother, Sir Charles Compton frequently operated out of Banbury. Another of the 2nd Earl's sons, Spencer, was captured in 1644, defending the family home of Compton Wynyates.

While modern Middleton Cheney is a single large village, in 1643 it was two distinct settlements. Centred on its 14th century church, Upper Middleton was the larger of the two, whilst Lower Middleton was only a small hamlet. The Bishops of Rochester owned both villages from the late 13th century onwards. The village we see today did not come into being until after 1913 when modern development filled the gap between the villages.[5] The extent of the 'Towne-field', a reference to the common field, mentioned in the sources is unknown for certain but may have encompassed the entire spur of land at the southern edge of both villages and was approximately 500 acres in size. On either side of the field were small valleys containing streams that drained into the River Cherwell. Most of the surrounding land was under cultivation in open field furlongs of ridge and furrow, much of which still survives in the current landscape. The old road from Banbury to Northampton, known as Banbury Lane, left the former town at the bridge, passed to the north of the village, and continued through Culworth until the 20th century bypass superseded it. The road to Bicester passed south of the Upper village through Lower Middleton and onwards to Kings Sutton and Astrop. Known as the 'Parsontide (Parsonage) Way', the main village street connected the former Priory at Chacombe with the Church at Kings Sutton.[6]

Southwest of the village was the Parish of Warkworth. Neither the Domesday Book nor the accounts of the reign of Henry II contain any reference to the village, and it was probably part of the Manor of Banbury. A chapel was built during the reign of Edward III to serve secular priests supplied by the Priory at Chacombe. The manor may have originated from this time and lay northwest of the church. In 1629 the manor house was purchased by the Holman family. Philip Holman (c.1593-1669), a London

---

[4] *A full Relation of the Siege of Banbury Castle by that Valiant and Faithfull Commander, Colonell Whetham, Governour of Northampton, now Commander-in-Chiefe in that Service, &c.* (BL/TT/E.8(9), London, 4 September, 1644.
[5] The Ordnance Survey map of 1888-1913 still shows two distinct villages with enclosed fields in-between.
[6] William Whellan & Co, *History, Gazetteer, and Directory of Northamptonshire; Comprising a general survey of the county*, (London, Whittaker and Co., 1749), p.631-32.

merchant, bought the manor for £14,000 and substantially rebuilt it. He was High-Sheriff of Northamptonshire in 1638 and sat on the Parliamentarian Committee for Northampton throughout the Civil War. The house eventually became neglected and difficult to maintain and was demolished in 1806.[7] The parish lay north of the road connecting the Parsontide Way with Banbury. A track led south from Warkworth (roughly following the line of the present Jurassic Way) to the ford to the East of Bodicote. At Warkworth, the track passed to the south of the church (possibly evidenced through field boundaries) before travelling northwards towards Middleton Cheney. It probably did not follow the current route of the footpath but joined the road into Middleton Cheney slightly to the east of the village. In the 17th century, a large part of the parish was either cultivated or in pasture, much like the present.

Fig.8 Warkworth Castle (1806)
The home of the Holman family,
who were notable Parliamentarians during the Civil War.
**(From a sketch by the Rev. W. Higginson,
reproduced in A History of Banbury, by William Potts)**

---

[7] Ibid, p.647-48

Fig.9 The grave slab of Sir Philip Holman.
Holman was Lord of the Manor of Warkworth and sat on the
Parliamentarian committee of Northampton.
(Author's photograph)

The Approach to Battle

On Wednesday, 3 May 1643, a great fire swept through the town of Banbury. According to Parliamentarian reports, the Royalists *'had maliciously set on fire & burnt a great part of the Towne, even at a time when no enemy approached it'*,[1] whilst another newspaper described the act as *'in a barbarous cruell manner.'*[2] The *Continuation of Certaine Speciall and remarkable Passages* gave further detail:

> *'...a hundred houses are burnt in Banbury, being sett on fire by the Cavaleers that are quartered there, for no other cause (as it is creditably informed) but because they did not pay the mony assessed upon them for the maintenance of the Kings Army.'* [3]

Whilst the Royalist sources are silent on this incident, the Parliamentarian accounts should not be taken at face value. The town was almost certainly uncooperative with the royal cause, given its strongly puritan leanings, but it would make little sense for the Royalists to burn it deliberately as it provided some means of taxation and supplies, and a deliberate burning down would also deny the Earl's men comfortable billets within the town. As an aside, at the end of its account of the battle, the Royalist *Mercurius Aulicus* added that the people of Banbury needed to be thankful that the King *'hath not burned to the ground this most wicked rebellious Towne.'*[4] This statement would not be logical if the town had already been extensively damaged. Fires were common in many towns and cities during the 17th century, and Banbury had been no exception. It is possible that the fire started accidentally, and the damage caused was not as extensive as reported. There are also reports of Royalist soldiers helping to put out the fire, which would appear contradictory had they started it.[5]

The importance of the fire is that it seems to have precipitated the Parliamentarian advance on Banbury and, therefore, the battle that followed. There are several different motivations given for the attack on Banbury, depending on the account consulted. One newspaper comments that *'they intended to be revenged on the Cavaliers for burning Banbury.'*[6] *Mercurius Civicus*, however, gives an entirely different reason for the attack launched against the town:

> *'A warrant was framed by the Cavaliers, counterfeiting his Excellencies the Earle of Essex his hand, and sent to Northampton, commanding those 500 Foot that were there, to meet his Forces at Banbury, which accordingly they intended to doe.'* [7]

---
[1] *Special Passages, Numb, 39.* (BL/TT/E.101(6).
[2] *A Perfect Diurnall, Numb. 47* (BL/TT/E.249(2))
[3] *A Continuation of Certaine Speciall and Remarkable Passages, Thursday the 4. of May. till Thursday the 11. of the same, 1643,* (BL/TT/E.249(2)).
[4] *Mercurius Aulicus, The Eighteenth Weeke*, Vol 1, p.257
[5] *A Continuation of Certaine Special and remarkable Passages,* (BL/TT/E.249(4).
[6] *A Perfect Diurnall, Numb.49.* (BL/TT/E.249(5).

Four other newsbooks followed in much the same vein, accusing the Royalists of forging a letter.[8] This looks like conspiracy journalism, and the accounts may have copied each other, but the Royalists had used such stratagems before as the 2nd Earl of Northampton had sent a forged letter to the garrison of Banbury before he seized the magazine in August 1642.[9] The use of such a letter was not, unsurprisingly, reported in the Royalist accounts until after the battle. Two weeks later, *Mercurius Aulicus* refuted the charge as 'unquestionably false', adding that the Parliamentarians *'hope to have the Towne betrayed unto them by some of the faithful men of Banbury.'*[10] The forged letter appears to be a Parliamentarian excuse to explain the defeat and attribute it to Royalist perfidiousness. On the other hand it was natural for the Royalists to refute an account that could attribute their success to dubious means and lessen the impact of their victory.

Intelligence received by Sir Samuel Luke, Scoutmaster to the Earl of Essex, at Newport Pagnell on 7 May gives us a different motivation. According to the report:

'That 6 troopes of Cavallyers coming on Friday last into Northamptonshire to plunder and pillage the contry, the peple understanding of it did rise, and sending to Northampton for some aid, beate them out of the contry, and pursued them as farr as Brackley, and have taken 6 peece of ordnance out of the towne of Northampton and intend to goe to take Banbury and to pull downe the castle.'[11]

The account does not specify where the raid was launched from but by implication the Parliamentarians must have believed it to be Banbury. The rising of the local population is also interesting for our story as it links to a recorded event immediately before the battle (see below, p42). The garrisons at Northampton and Banbury frequently raided each other's territory so why this particular raid galvanised the Parliamentarians to make a retaliatory attack is unknown. Perhaps, for the Parliamentarians at least, this was a raid too far and also an opportunity to retaliate with the support of the local population who had come out against the Royalists.

---

[7] *Mercurius Civicus, Numb 1*, p.12.
[8] *Certaine Informations, Numb.17*, E.101(24). *A Perfect Diurnall, Numb.48.* (BL/TT/E.249(3). *A Perfect Diurnall*, Numb.49. (BL/TT/E.249(5). *A Continuation of Certaine Special and remarkable Passages, Num.44*, (BL/TT/E.249(4). The *Continuation* reported that the Northamptonshire forces received 'misinformation'. *A Perfect Diurnall number 49* states that the letter was sent from Prince Rupert ordering the Northamptonshire forces to join him at Reading. This seems unrealistic given the distances covered, the proximity to the Oxford Army near Reading and that Banbury was obviously the intended target. *Number 48* says that the Northamptonshire forces were to attack Banbury in concert with an attack to be launched on Oxford by the Earl of Essex. The *Certaine Informations* reported that Essex intended to send some of his own men to meet them at Banbury.
[9] *The Earle of Portlands Charge, Being the relation of the Earle of Northamptons surprizing the Magazine at Banbury by the forging of a false Letter.* (BL/TT/E.110(8))
[10] *Mercurius Aulicus, The Twentieth Weeke, Vol I*, p.289
[11] I.G.Philip. p.71

Fig.10 Banbury Lane. This photograph shows part of the Lane, which is still visible as a track near Grumblers Holt, Moreton Pinckney.
(Author's Photograph)

Finally, we must consider whether the Parliamentarians had designs to permanently occupy the castle after its capture and install a garrison rather than just slighting it. This was an attractive proposition as the capture of the castle would threaten the Royalist position in north Oxfordshire. A Parliamentarian garrison would then also be able to sit astride the Royalists lines of communication with the North Midlands. Whether the Parliamentarians would be able to accomplish this given the situation in May 1643 is debatable. They were unable to take the castle during the siege of 1644 with a greater number of troops and even larger resources. The Banbury garrison was a thorough nuisance to the Northamptonshire Parliamentarians and although no source mentions a permanent occupation it was probably not far from the thoughts of the Northamptonshire Committee.

It is, given the number of motivations discussed above, difficult to ascertain the real reason for the attack launched on Banbury as any of the above motivations would be valid. It may be that the raid represented pure opportunism on the side of the

Parliamentarians, designed to take advantage of any Royalist confusion following the fire. The reports of the garrison withdrawing may have also been an extra inducement.

The exact route of the march of the Parliamentarians is not mentioned in the sources, but it was undoubtedly along Banbury Lane. This was an old medieval drovers' road which connected Banbury with Northampton.[12] It was also the most direct route between the two towns and was the route taken by the rebel army and later their reinforcements at the battle of Edgcote in 1469.[13] What was true in 1469 would still be pertinent in 1643. Only by using the shortest and most direct route could the Parliamentarians hope to surprise the town. Only one village, Culworth, is mentioned in the sources. This adds weight to the Parliamentarians advancing along Banbury Lane as Culworth sits directly astride the road as it makes its way towards Banbury. From Culworth, the lane drops down to Thorpe Mandeville and, from there, moves towards the bridge over the river Cherwell. Shortly after Thorpe Mandeville, the Parsontide Way crosses Banbury Lane, allowing for a turn-off to Middleton Cheney. It was at Culworth that the Parliamentarians decided to concentrate their forces. The first troops may have reached the village on 5 May.[14] The main route from Northampton crossed the river Nene to the south. Once over the river, the Parliamentarians would pass through Towcester and on to Culworth via Wappenham and Weston. We cannot even be sure that the Parliamentarian force marched as one body. The *Speciall Passages* noted that 150 marched on Thursday and another 120 foot and three troops of horse arrived the next day.[15] Having concentrated his force on Friday, 5 May, the Parliamentarian commander would be able to rest his men ready for the forthcoming attack on Banbury.

Before looking further at the Parliamentarian advance on Banbury, it is worth examining the account in *A Perfect Diurnall,* which narrates a different version of events:

> '...he that commanded in chiefe, had intelligence of three Ambuscadoes of horse in his March, and therefore commanded a retreat, but the Countrey people complaying of their being drawne heretofore and had lost their labour, did resolve to do somewhat before they would returne, well they went on according to their resolution, and beat up the first Ambuscado who fled to the second...' [16]

---

[12] M W Brown, M.A. *Northamptonshire (Cambridge County Geographies),* (Cambridge, University Press, 1911), p.150.

[13] Evans, Graham *The Battle of Edgcote 1469 - Re-evaluating the evidence,* (Northampton Battlefields Society, 2019), pp.34/36/39. Brooks, Richard, *Cassells Battlefield of Britain and Ireland,* (London, Weidenfeld & Nicholson, 2005), pp.255-7. Both Brooks and Evans stress the importance of Banbury Lane as a main artery of communication.

[14] *Speciall Passages, Numb.40.* in Beesley, fn.32. p.377. The summary mentions that the troops arrived on two specific days

[15] *Speciall Passages, Numb.40* in Beesley, p.347.

[16] *A Perfect Diurnall Numb.48,* (BL/TT/E.249(6).

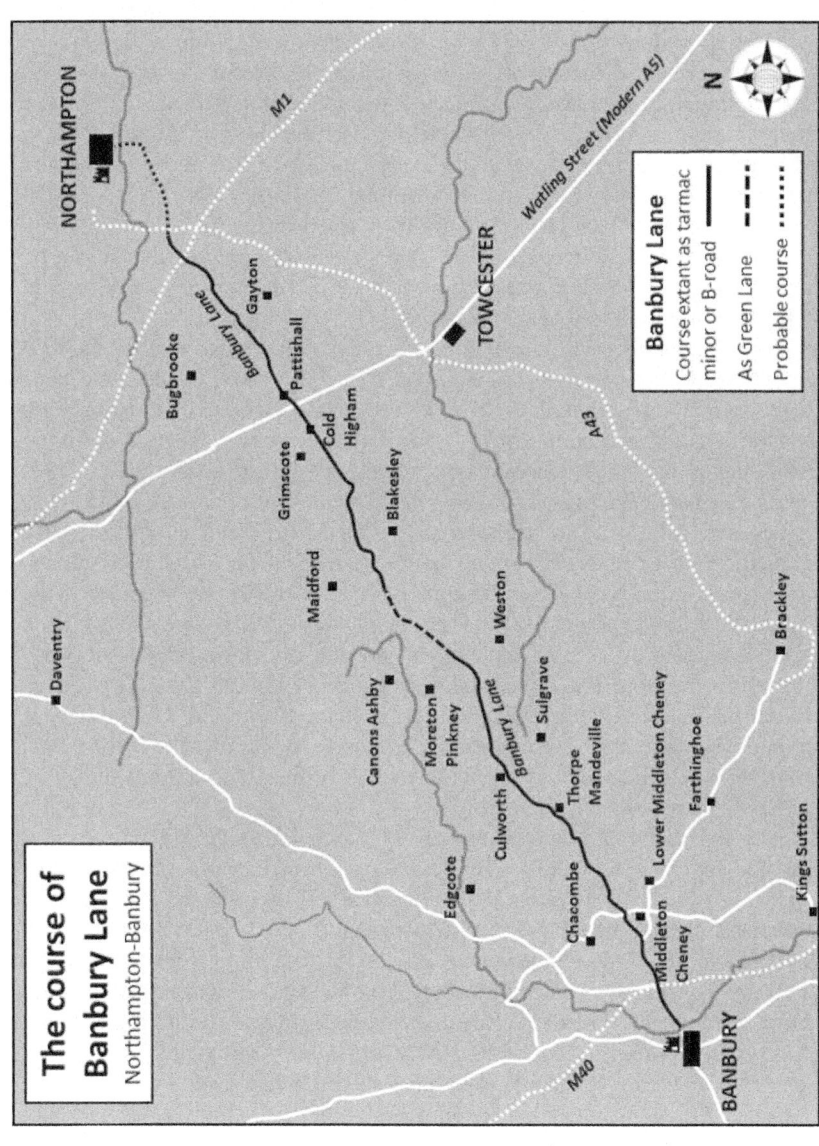

Map.4 Banbury Lane - the probable route of the Parliamentarians from Northampton to Middleton Cheney. **(Map by the Author)**

A Perfect Diurnall's account is the only source that claims the local inhabitants were involved in the battle. To obtain intelligence, the Earl would have either relied upon local informants, or sent out scouts to report on the enemy's movements. It may have been these scouting parties that were set upon by the local people. Alternatively, these men could have been detachments of the regiment quartered in the local villages. Once the Parliamentarians were near enough to assist, the local population could have felt confident enough to attempt to evict them. An alternative explanation is that the author had heard of the intelligence given to Sir Samuel Luke (see above, p. 40) and added these details immediately before the battle rather than at an earlier date. A further source alleges that the Royalists surprised the Parliamentarians as they were marching towards Banbury, while *A Continuation of Certaine Special and remarkable Passages*, also makes this claim.[17] These accounts of a surprise attack and the story of the forged letter play into the narrative of Royalist duplicity.

Having decided to launch his attack, the Parliamentarian commander led his men out of Culworth towards Banbury. Direct access into the town would have been possible by crossing the bridge over the river Cherwell, but there were problems with this route. The first obstacle would have been the bridge itself. It could easily be barricaded or even broken before anyone could even arrive. More importantly, it was dominated by the castle. The Royalists could easily have sited their artillery to cover the approaches, thus making an assault very costly. If a direct assault across the bridge was impractical, another means of crossing the river needed to be found. Crossing the river north or south of the town would be a possibility but the nearest crossing to the north was the bridge at Cropredy. To the south there was a ford at Kings Sutton and, two miles south of Banbury, there was another opposite Bodicote. We do not know how much intelligence the Parliamentarians had obtained about the river and its crossing points. The local landowner, Philip Holman, sat on the Committee of Northampton during the war. Given the ford's proximity to his house at Warkworth, it would be surprising if he had not passed on some information or appointed a guide who knew the local crossing points.

There are hints that, notwithstanding any advice from Holman, the Parliamentarians reconnoitred the approaches to the bridge at Banbury as one Royalist account claims that they managed to get *'within half a mile of the town'*.[18] This suggests that some of the Parliamentarian scouts may have reached Grimsbury, now a suburb of Banbury on the eastern side of the river, to report on events at the bridge and were immediately detected, thus giving the Earl advanced warning of the Parliamentarian approach. They may also have encountered some of the Royalists' outlying pickets. With a large enemy force in the area, it would have been foolish had the Earl not ordered some form of defence against an attack on the bridge from the east bank of the Cherwell. Seeing the bridge defended, the scouts may have returned to the main body to suggest an

---

[17] *A Perfect Diurnall, Numb.49.* (BL/TT/E.249(5). *A Continuation of Certaine Special and remarkable Passages, Numb.44,* (BL/TT/E.249(4).
[18] Warburton, Vol.II, p.186.

alternative route to bypass it. The ford at Bodicote was the next nearest crossing and would allow the Parliamentarians to sweep up from the south and attack Banbury without requiring a passage across the bridge.

To reach the ford from Culworth, the Parliamentarians would have advanced down the Banbury Lane until it met the old Parsontide Way north of Middleton Cheney village. The Parsontide Way was a track which had formerly linked the old priory at Chacombe with the parish church at Kings Sutton. Why the road should connect the two sites is unknown, but Kings Sutton had belonged to the English kings as far back as Alfred the Great. The church also had one of its ecclesiastical courts within the village.[19] Although only a track, this would be suitable for the drake and its fore-carriage limber to manoeuvre along. The Parliamentarians would also have the advantage of keeping to the high ground along the spur heading off to the south of Middleton Cheney at the start of their march. The cavalry would have led the advance to the ford with the main body and the drake following.

Two different routes lay ahead of the Parliamentarians once they descended from the spur. The first option was to turn towards Warkworth and follow the track down to the ford. Alternatively, they could take the more direct route to the ford by marching straight across the fields. The advantage of the terrain here is that it is relatively flat and ideal for the movement of wagons and artillery. The advance probably crossed the fields on the same line as the disused railway between Bicester and Banbury, which followed the base of a series of spurs jutting out into the river valley. The ground between the dismantled railway and the ford would have looked different in 1643 as the building of the railway and the modern M40 motorway has disturbed the landscape. Had the Parliamentarians descended from the track, they may have had a clearer view of what awaited them. We do not know how near to the ford they managed to advance or whether they

Fig.11 The ford at Bodicote during a dry season. The ford would have presented few obstacles to Cavalry or foot wishing to cross.
(Photo: Nicholas Haynes)

---

[19] Roger Bellamy, *The Church of St. Peter and St. Paul, A Historical Guide*. Church booklet: https://www.kingssutton.org/static/content-uploads/pdfs/2013/07/22/Church_History_Final_Colour.pdf. [Accessed 20 November 2020], p.9.

halted on a spur of high ground three-quarters of a mile short of the ford, which gave a better view of the terrain ahead. The cavalry may have moved forward to inspect the ford before allowing the foot and cannon to cross. In either case a most unwelcome sight awaited them on the high ground on the other side of the river.

Fig.12 The Parsontide Way near the battlefield. Originally this led from Chacombe Priory to the church at Kings Sutton. The Parliamentarians used this route to advance towards the ford at Bodicote.
(Author's Photograph)

Fig.13 The floodplain from near the ford at Bodicote. The Parliamentarians probably advanced through the centre of the picture on their way to the ford.
(Author's Photograph)

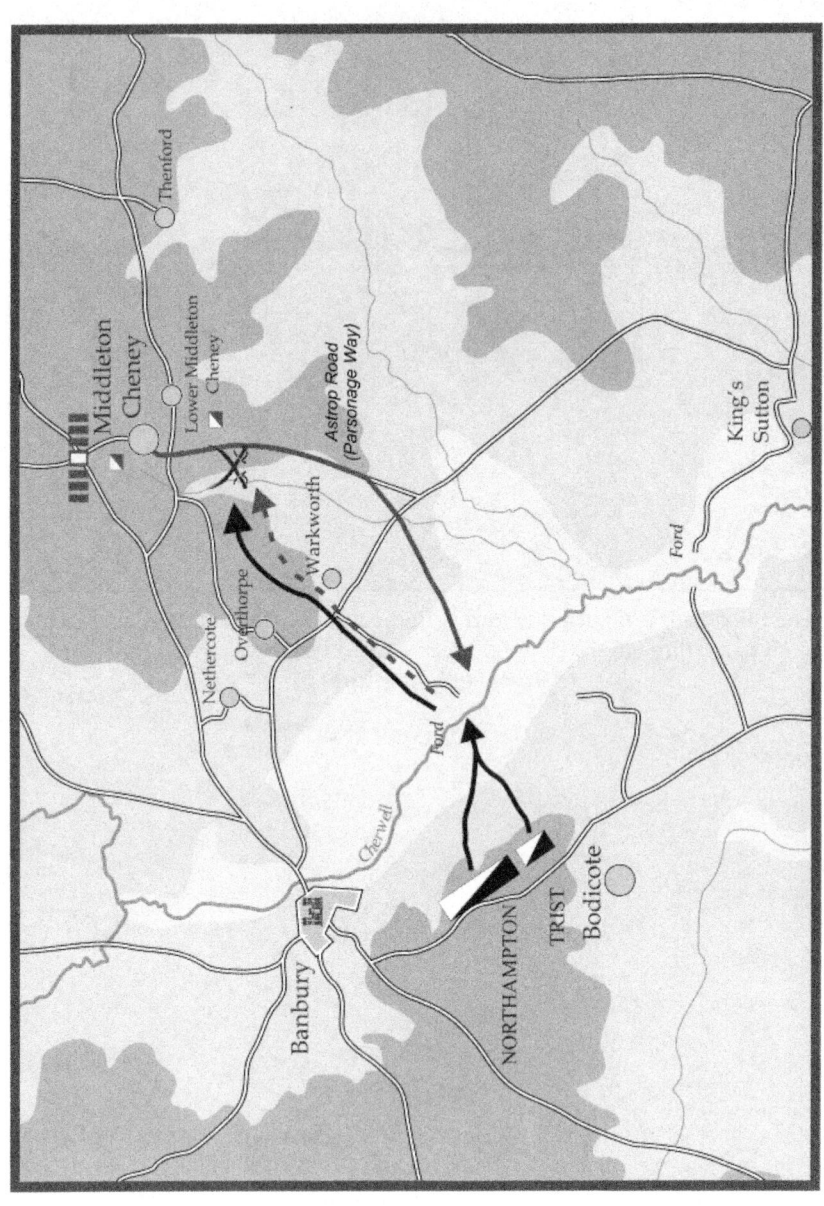

Map.5 The conjectural movements of the Royalist and Parliamentarian forces on 6th May 1643. **(Map by © Nick Lipscombe)**

The Earl Counterattacks

Considering Culworth's proximity to Banbury, it is strange that the Earl of Northampton did not receive any news of the Parliamentarian concentration the day before. By midday, according to *Mercurius Aulicus*, the Earl had received notification of the Parliamentarian advance:

> 'About twelve of the clocke today, my Lord had certaine notice of the Rebells being at Culworth, whereupon my Lord drew out his forces towards Bodicot within a mile of Banbury...' [1]

Despite the possible rumours that the Royalists had withdrawn to Oxford, at least three regiments were present in the Banbury area. The Earl of Northampton's foot regiment was garrisoning the castle, which left him only his own horse regiment and that of the Prince of Wales with which to oppose the advancing Parliamentarians.

The Earl's main concern at this point was to decide which route the enemy would most likely take to advance upon the town. Had he been confident that the Parliamentarians were aiming to cross Banbury bridge, he would undoubtedly have kept his horse nearer to the town. By moving onto the high ground between Bodicote and Banbury, he would be able to cover the ford and also be able to react to any attack on the bridge. Once the Earl had located the Parliamentarians, he sent Captain Trist *'to face them and to keep them in action.'* [2] He had already decided to engage the Parliamentarians to remove the threat to Banbury. The immediate problem was that a river lay between him and the enemy located on the opposite side.

The Parliamentarians, now viewing a large body of horse on the opposite ridge, may have decided that it was time to retreat towards Middleton Cheney. The terrain at this point was unsuitable for a cavalry engagement and there may have been boggy ground either side of the river. The Cherwell was also an obstacle which the Royalists had to contend with and to cross it the Earl would have had to form his men into a column which would be vulnerable to Parliamentarian attack. It would also have taken some time for the entire Royalist force to cross the river by which time the Parliamentarians might have managed to slip away before they could be engaged. To prevent this, the Earl sent Captain Trist with a small force to keep the enemy occupied while he followed with his main body. To engage them, Trist would have needed to cross the ford facing the enemy and if the Parliamentarians had managed to reach the riverbank they would have been in a position to prevent this. By blocking the ford at the riverbank and using the drake to cover the crossing, the Royalists would have had difficulty crossing the river. Trist, therefore, must have been able to cross the ford without opposition which implies that the Parliamentarians halted before they reached

---

[1] *Mercurius Aulicus, The Eighteenth Weeke,* Vol 1, p.257.
[2] *Ibid*, p.257

the river. Given the disparity in numbers, Trist was only to engage the Parliamentarians enough to slow their retreat without putting his force in danger. Whilst described as a 'party', Trist probably had at least half of the Prince's regiment with him. While this would not been able to inflict much damage to the retiring enemy, it would be enough to keep Trist from being overwhelmed.

Fig.14 The view towards the initial Royalist position on the ridge at Bodicote where the Earl of Northampton deployed his brigade before advancing over the ford.
(Author's Photograph)

Trist was undoubtedly an experienced soldier. A Royalist account notes that:

'...the Capt, performed so well & souldierlike that he put the enemy into a posture of retreatings...' [3]

These manoeuvres would have involved Trist engaging the rear-guard of the retreating troops to his front. When Trist attacked, the Parliamentarian horse would be obliged to stand in order to fend off attacks, allowing the infantry to retire unmolested. There is no account of Trist attacking the Parliamentarians, and his role at this stage was only to maintain contact until the Earl arrived with the remainder of

[3] *Ibid* p.257.

the brigade. The advantage of this tactic for the Royalists was that it would have kept the opposing cavalry busy trying to cover the foot while also ensuring that they were unable to detect the main Royalist cavalry force which was moving forward. We do not know the direction of the retreat, but two different routes were available. Depending on where the Parliamentarians halted, they may have chosen to retreat directly towards Warkworth. The track heading back towards the village still exists today as a farm track, although it appears to have stopped at the road between Banbury and Kings Sutton. Looking at a modern map, a series of field boundaries and footpaths may show that the track continued to the west of the hamlet on a straight course before joining the Banbury to Middleton Cheney lane on the western side of the village. Alternatively, the Parliamentarians could withdraw the same way they arrived and retreat along the Parsontide Way.

Fig.15 The view towards Warkworth and Middleton Cheney from the ridge at Bodicote.
(Photo: Nicholas Haynes)

Whilst Trist followed the retreating Parliamentarians, the route taken by the remainder of the Earl's command is unknown. One course available to him was to take his men back through Banbury and cross the river at the bridge. From here, they could have proceeded along Banbury Lane and advanced upon the village from the west. The advantage of this route meant they could have approached the Parliamentarians from a different and unexpected direction to surprise them. However, there were dangers in choosing this course of action. An experienced commander would not have divided his force in the face of the enemy unless circumstances dictated that there was no other option. Even if Trist did have a slight superiority, there was always the danger that his opponent could stand and turn to try and eliminate his small force before the rest of the brigade arrived. Whilst Trist's small party should easily have been able to evade an opponent primarily composed of foot, this was still a possibility. Until the Earl was certain by which route the enemy was retreating, he would have remained at Bodicote. Having ascertained that the Parliamentarians were retiring towards Middleton Cheney, the main body would probably have crossed over the ford and followed Captain Trist. The Earl would likely have preferred this option as he could keep in contact with Trist. Since his entire force was composed of cavalry, he would also have the speed to cut north back to Banbury if the Parliamentarians moved in that direction. Although the route taken by both sides must remain conjecture, it was perhaps inevitable that the Parliamentarian commander, constantly harassed by Trist's troopers, finally decided to make a stand with the knowledge that the Earl was approaching.

The Main Engagement

Nothing in the sources suggests why the Parliamentarians decided to fight at Middleton Cheney. The Parliamentarian commander probably decided that with the main Royalist body not yet engaged, his column might face destruction if he attempted to retreat to Northampton. If the Royalists continued their harrying, there was a risk that the column would be overwhelmed with disastrous results. He may have judged he could win the forthcoming engagement with his superiority in infantry along with the single artillery piece to support him. The exact location of the battle is not known for certain. As with most minor Civil War actions, a range of alternatives are possible. The lack of detailed topographic description in the sources also hinders locating the area of fighting. The only clue is in *Mercurius Aulicus,* who wrote that the Royalists:

> *'...found the enemy in a close body of Middleton Cheney Towne field, where they made a stand...'* [1]

The exact location and dimensions of the 'Towne field' is unknown. It may have encompassed the entire area of land on top of the spur to the south of both villages (see Map. 3). Middleton Cheney practised an open-field farming system well into the 18th century. The common fields of the parish were not enclosed until an Act of Parliament in 1769 and the Enclosure Map of 1770 shows the open areas, pathways and the ridge and furrow, which are still in evidence today.[2] One account states that the initial position was on a hill three miles from Banbury.[3] The spur is approximately 2.5 miles from the town and is the most prominent feature in the area, which adds some weight to this being the correct battlefield location.

Traditionally, the battle was said to have been fought in a location at Moors Drive. Now a built-up area, this would have been at the most northern point of the Town Field abutting the village's southern end. The ideal terrain to arrange a defence would have been along the edge of the spur (deployment 'A', Map 6, overleaf). The steepness of the slope would provide an excellent defensive position which would give a good view back towards Banbury and provide some protection. From the top of the spur, the slope drops steeply down into a small valley containing a stream which would prove an obstacle, if only a minor one. On the opposite side of the stream, the slope rises again to a ridge of high ground (see Fig.18 p60). The Parliamentarians may have deployed their men at the top of the hill, with part of the cavalry deployed in the area of Moors

---

[1] *Mercurius Aulicus, The Eighteenth Weeke,* Vol 1, p.257. James Heath also describes the battle as being in the 'Town Field' however his chronicle was written forty two years later in 1675. He most likely got the name from *Mercurius Aulicus'* account of the battle.
[2] 'Middleton Cheney', in *An Inventory of the Historical Monuments in the County of Northamptonshire, Volume 4, Archaeological Sites in South-West Northamptonshire* (London, 1982), pp. 101-102. British History Online http://www.british-history.ac.uk/rchme/northants/vol4/pp101-102 [accessed 8 January 2021].
[3] *Special Passages, Num.40.* in Beesley, fn.32, p.347.

Drive.[4] The other cavalry were probably deployed on the left wing to oppose any Royalist move up the spur at that point. The position of the drake is unknown, although it may have been on the right where it could help cover the stream crossing.

Some finds that were reputed to have come from the battle have been found in the village. A sword discovered in the early 20th century in a wall in Royal Oak Lane, which was part of Lower Middleton Cheney, is said to be from the time of the battle. The Church also displayed a cannonball from 'the battle of the Moors'. It was reputed to weigh 14lb which, if of the period, would be more appropriate for a siege piece and clearly not fired by the 6 pounder drake. It may have been lost by the main Royalist army when it passed through before the battle of Cropredy Bridge. These reports of finds should be treated with care as they have now disappeared and cannot be firmly corroborated.[5]

Analysing the routes that lead to the battlefield may also help determine the site. If the Parliamentarians had withdrawn through Warkworth, they would have reached the village along the main Banbury to Brackley road. They could choose to cover the area where the road crossed a stream on the village's western side, north of the deployment shown at 'A' on Map 6. The main road into the village could be barred here, with the stream presenting an obstacle for the opposing cavalry. If the Parliamentarians were drawn up in the traditional formation of infantry in the centre and cavalry on the wings, this location would have problems. Whilst it would be an ideal position for the foot and artillery to cover the crossing, deploying the cavalry would be difficult. Although we do not know the precise extent of the village in 1643, the church and other buildings would have lined the High Street. Any cavalry on the right wing would be fighting in a very constricted area with houses and other structures behind them. Alternatively, if the retreat had followed the Parsontide Way, the Parliamentarians might have chosen to make their stand across the spur as it traversed south of the village (deployment 'B', Map 6). Here they would be able to block the Royalist advance, but whilst the flat terrain was advantageous for cavalry, the steep slopes would restrict their manoeuvrability on either side of the spur. As the Royalists were composed entirely of cavalry, they did not need to defend a static position and could therefore envelop the Parliamentarian line.

There is limited information as to when the engagement started. The only clue, again in *Mercurius Aulicus*, is that the Earl received notice of the enemy concentrating their forces at midday in Culworth. It takes at least two to two and a half hours to walk from Culworth to the ford at Bodicote. The drake and accompanying wagons would probably have slowed down the march. Assuming the Parliamentarians did not reach

---

[4] The now built up areas south of the road including Moors Drive, The Avenue and Horton Road did not exist at the time of the battle and were built in the 20th century. The wooded areas along the stream and around Moors Drive also did not exist until post-1913. *Ordnance Survey 6 inch to 1 mile Old Map (1888-1913) of Middleton Cheney, Northamptonshire.*

[5] Leonard W. Jerrams, *A Brief History of Middleton Cheney, Northamptonshire with Childhood Memories,* (1984)

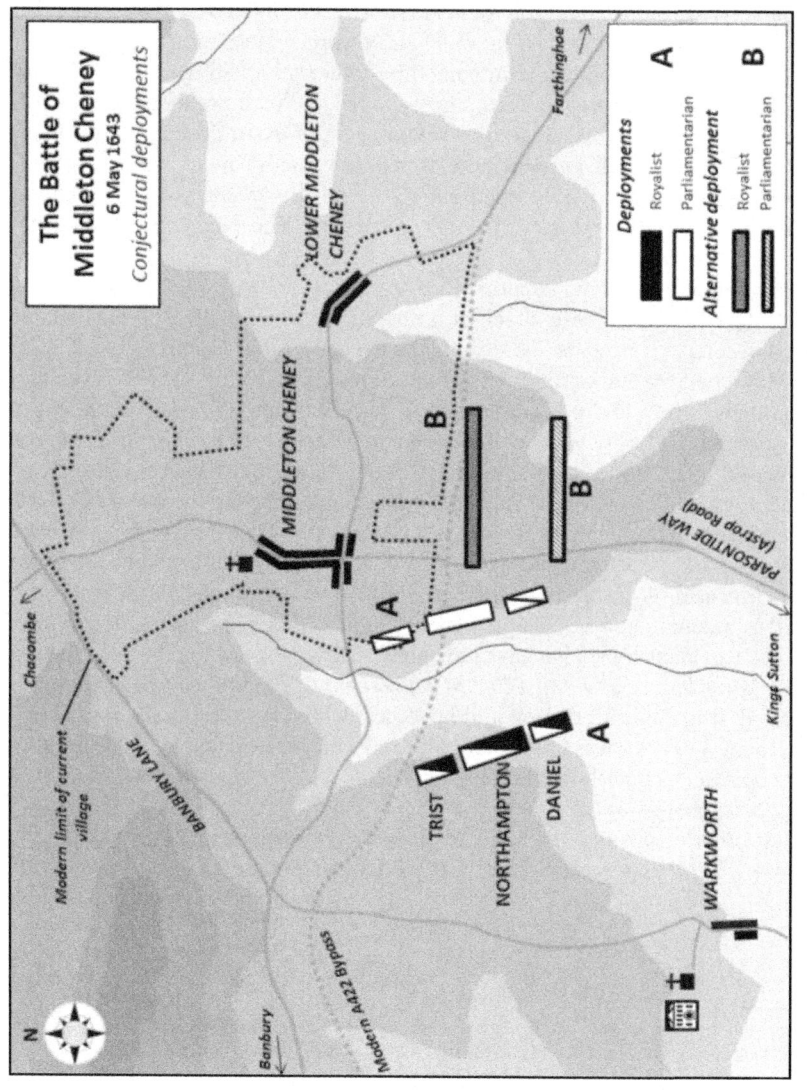

Map.6 Conjectural and alternative deployments of the Royalist and Parliamentarian forces (**Map by the Author**)

the ford itself and allowing time for them to retreat to Middleton Cheney, the battle could not have started until the middle of the afternoon at the earliest. It appears, however, to have been a short affair. *A Continuation* notes that *'they* [the Parliamentarians] *were surprised by a great party of the enemy's horse'*[6] whilst another version says that the Royalists *'fell on them suddaynly'*.[7] Here the author could be implying that the defeat resulted from something other than bad leadership. Whilst claiming the element of surprise, it would give the reader the impression that this was not a fair fight and the Royalists had to use cunning, surprise or deception to achieve victory. The *Speciall Passages* attribute the defeat to the incompetence of the Parliamentarian commander who *'contrary to the opinion of others, ordered his forces to descend into the valley, where they were defeated'*.[8] The other accounts do not confirm this version of events.

The Parliamentarians, having formed up, appear to have awaited the oncoming Royalists. Rather than a surprise attack or going straight into battle, the Earl waited until he had ordered his brigade. To do this, he needed to join Captain Trist and his men. Once together, the Earl split his force into three parts. He divided the Prince of Wales' regiment in half and placed it on the wings with the two most experienced officers in command. Major Daniel commanded on the right, whilst Captain Trist took charge of the left. The Earl kept his regiment in the centre under his overall control, probably deploying his men on the ridge of high ground opposite the enemy line. He began the engagement by ordering the first attack probably advancing his line forward to start closing on the Parliamentarians. According to a Royalist account, the drake came into action as it *'gave fire upon his Lordship : with their brasse peece 3 severall times'*.[9] A Parliamentarian account agreed that *'the Cannonier shot three shot with his Drake.'*[10] The Royalists must also have advanced within range of the Parliamentarian foot as they *'gave him a very hot volley of Musket shot'*.[11] Had the Parliamentarians been surprised, it is doubtful they would have been able to get the drake into action before the Royalist cavalry was upon them. The drake may have caused some casualties amongst the Royalists, one shot unhorsing *'a gallant Sparke whom men suppose to be the Young Earle of Northampton.'*[12]

The first order of business for the Royalists was to disperse the Parliamentarian horse. *Mercurius Aulicus* implies that all of the Royalist horse took part in this first charge:

---

[6] *A Continuation of certain Speciall and Remarkable Passages, from Thursday the 6. of May, till Thursday the 11. of May, 1643*, (BL/TT/E.101(17).

[7] *A Continuation of Certaine Speciall and Remarkable Passages, from Thursday the 4. of May. till Thursday the 11. Of the same, 1643*, (BL/TT/E.249(4). Also *A Perfect Diurnall, Numb.49.* (BL/TT/E.249(5).

[8] *Special Passages, Numb.40.* in Beesley fn.32, p.347.

[9] *Mercurius Aulicus, The Eighteenth Weeke,* Vol 1, p.257.

[10] *A Perfect Diurnall Numb.48,* BL/TT/E.249(6).

[11] *Mercurius Aulicus, The Eighteenth Weeke,* Vol 1, p.257.

[12] *A Perfect Diurnall Numb.48,* (BL/TT/E.249(6).

Fig.16 A view of the battlefield from the Royalist forming up position.
(Author's Photograph)

Fig.17 The Parliamentarian position at the top of the slope.
The picture gives a good idea of the steepness of the terrain.
(Author's Photograph)

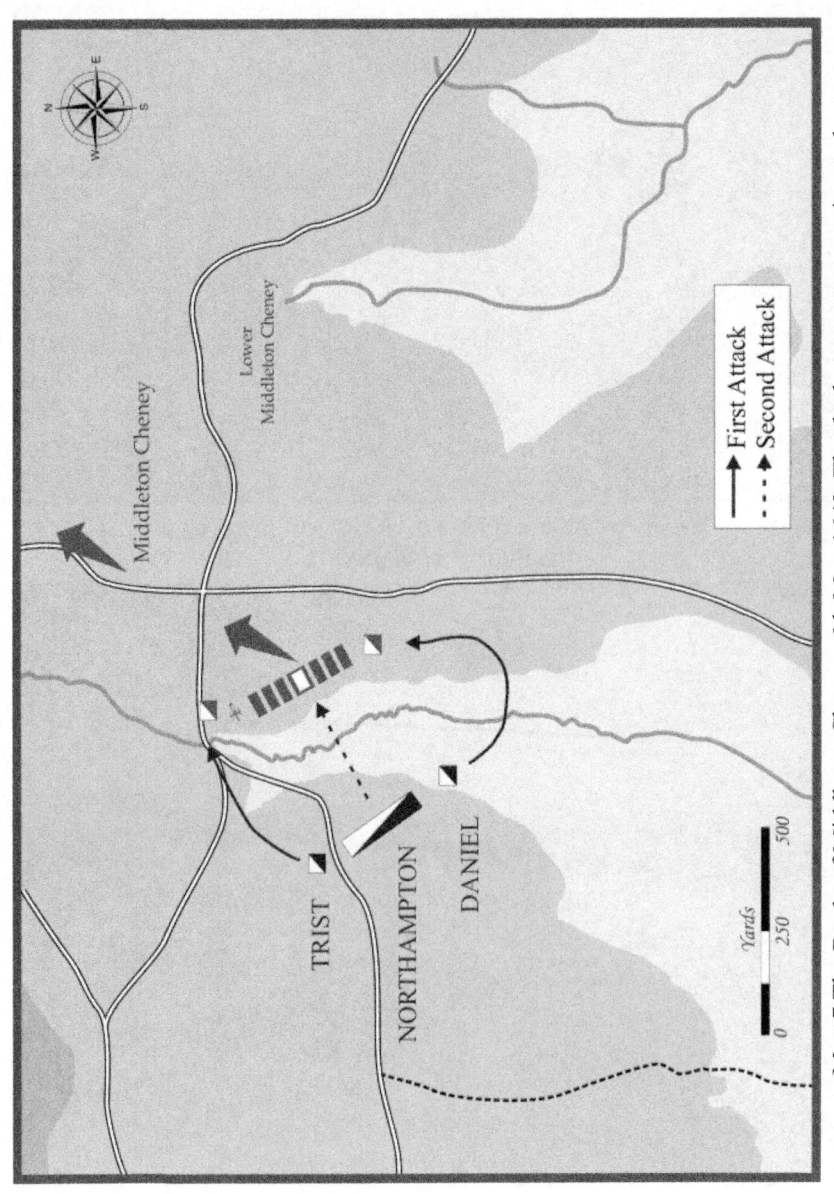

Map.7 The Battle of Middleton Cheney, 6th May 1643. The deployments are conjectural. (**Map by © Nick Lipscombe**)

'His Lordship charged them on the front, Sergeant Major Daniel on the right wing, & Cap. Trist on the left: some of my Lords horse pursued theirs, killed & tooke many of them, yet the rest were so fleet that they escaped in small companies into by-lanes and hedges and ranne to Northampton...' [13]

A Perfect Diurnall, although writing in the context of an ambush, noted that the Cavaliers *'charged our men at which charge all our Horse ranne away.'* [14] We do not know whether the Earl committed all his troopers to the first charge. However, he probably had some confidence that the Parliamentarian foot would not be able to move swiftly and escape before he could return to deal with them. In this instance he did not make the mistake that the Royalist horse had made in previous battles. Instead of allowing his men to continue pursuing the retreating enemy horse, he rallied them and led them back onto the battlefield. The foot must have known what was about to happen. As the Earl recalled his men back onto the field, he launched a second charge aimed at the now abandoned foot. Only two accounts mention this second charge. *A Perfect Diurnall* wrote that *'at the second charge the foote were routed and every man shifted for himself.'* [15] The Royalist account merely states that the foot was *'wholly routed'*.[16] The formation appears to have fallen apart immediately, and it was every man for himself.

In theory, the foot should have been able to stand, at least for longer than it did. The musketeers may only have been able to fire a few volleys before they retreated under the protection of their own pikemen which the Royalist horse could not approach due to their long pikes. If the Royalists had been unable to break into the Parliamentarian ranks, then there was every chance that they may have eventually decided to withdraw. The most plausible explanation therefore, is that the Northampton foot, which was a garrison unit, was not experienced enough to fight against the more experienced Royalist horse for a protracted period of time. They may have suffered a catastrophic collapse of morale with the disappearance of their supporting horse. With the formation breaking apart, there would be little to stop the Royalists from penetrating the Parliamentarian ranks and cutting down the fleeing soldiers. Those men that could escape probably fled through Middleton Cheney, although most, if not all, were probably rounded up and taken prisoner by the victorious Royalists. With the destruction of the Parliamentarian foot, the battle was over.

---

[13] *Mercurius Aulicus, The Eighteenth Weeke,* Vol 1, p.257.
[14] *A Perfect Diurnall Numb.48,*(BL/TT/E.249(6).
[15] Ibid
[16] *Mercurius Aulicus, The Eighteenth Weeke,* Vol 1, p.257.

Fig.18 Part of the battlefield viewed from the Parliamentarian position in the Town Field. The Royalists would have deployed on the far side of the valley.
(Author's Photograph)

Fig.19 The Town Field adjacent to Moors Drive.
Much of the fighting would have taken place here, in the adjacent fields and in the now built-up area south of the village.
(Author's Photograph)

The Aftermath

The battle's immediate effect was removing the threat to Banbury. The Earl of Northampton could now focus his attention on the impending munitions convoy. Moreover, he had completed his victory with few casualties to his force. The Parliamentarians, however, had suffered significant losses. Assessing casualties for battles of this period can be challenging because of the wide variance within the sources. Authors inflated or minimised the losses depending on their personal bias or intended audience. The Royalist *Mercurius Aulicus* reported:

'killed 217 of them upon the place and tooke above 300 prisoners....there were Banbury men amongst these Rebels, & many of them lay dead in the field; there were divers Captaines and commanders taken, Captaine Martin, Captaine Melvin a Scottish man, with others.'[1]

Philip Willoughby's letter to Prince Rupert, on the morning directly after the battle, stated that the Royalists:

'hath taken three hundred prisoners, killed above a hundred in the place, wounded most of the rest.'[2]

The Earl of Clarendon wrote some years later that there were *'killed above 200 of their foot, and took as many more prisoners.'* Here though, he may have been writing either from the memory of Willoughby's letter read at court or borrowed from *Mercurius Aulicus*' account. The newspaper may also have used Willoughby's letter as its primary source, although the count of 217 is a specific number and may have come from discussions with someone at the battle. Clarendon added that most of the Parliamentarians *'whereof were shrewdly hurt, the young Earl that day sacrificing to the memory of his father.'*[3] Considering the large number of casualties, anyone reading his account might conclude that some form of a massacre had taken place. It also implied that the Earl had ordered his men to take revenge on the Parliamentarians for his father's death at Hopton Heath. Clarendon's recollections of what happened or what he was told may have been unclear. However enraged the young Earl may have been about his father's death, this sort of behaviour would be most uncharacteristic, and he never displayed signs of this during his long Civil War service. The range of Parliamentarians killed in the fighting given by the Royalist accounts is from 100 to 217. They also list 300 prisoners. As for their own casualties, Willoughby recorded that there were only three killed on the Royalist side. The same was reported by

---
[1] *Mercurius Aulicus, The Eighteenth Weeke,* Vol 1, p.257
[2] Warburton, *Vol.II*, p.186.
[3] Clarendon, Edward Hyde, 1st Earl of, *The History of the Rebellion and Civil Wars in England,* (Oxford, Oxford University Press, 1843), p.388.

Mercurius Aulicus, which added that there were *'none of any note, nor any officer so much as hurt save onely Major Daniell had a slight hurt in the Legge.'*

In contrast the Parliamentarian London newspapers quote a higher figure for the number of Royalists slain. Two of the Parliamentarian accounts put the number of killed at 30. One of these stated that the drake caused all of these casualties. This number should be treated with caution but not dismissed out of hand. The Banbury burial register records that on 8 May, there was buried a *'soldiar of Captain Clark's'*.[4] Captain Matthew Clarke was in command of a troop of horse in the Earl of

Table 2
Royalist and Parliamentarian casualties at Middleton Cheney*

Source	Parliamentarian	Royalist
Mercurius Aulicus (R)	217 killed 300 prisoners	3 killed Few wounded
Philip Willoughby (R)	100+ killed 300 prisoners	3 killed
Clarendon's History (R)	200 killed 200+ prisoners	
Certain Informations, 17 (P)	40 killed 60 prisoners	
A Perfect Diurnall, 49 (P)	50 killed 300 prisoners	
A Perfect Diurnall, 48 (P)	20 killed 100 prisoners	30 killed
A Continuation 44 (P)	30 killed	30 killed
Middleton Cheney Parish Register	46 burials	
Banbury Parish Burial Register	5 - 7** burials	
James Heath (1675)	200 killed 300 prisoners	

*Four editions of the London newspapers reported Parliamentarian casualties. *A Perfect Diurnall, Numb.48, A Perfect Diurnall, Numb.49,* and *A Continuation of Certaine Speciall and Remarkable Passages from both Houses of Parliament, and other Parts of the Kingdom. From Thursday the 4. of May. till Thursday the 11. of the same, 1643, Numb. 44. A Continuation* has possibly confused the skirmishes at Bicester and Middleton Cheney so its figures should be treated with caution.

** Burials between 7-25 May who may not all have been casualties from Middleton Cheney

---

[4] *Baptism and Burial Register of Banbury, Oxfordshire, Part One, 1558-1653*, (Ed. J.S.W.Gibson), (Oxford, The Banbury Historical Society Vol.7, 1966), p.238-39. Stuart Reid, *Officers and Regiments of the Royalist Army*, Volume 3, I-Q, (Newthorpe, Partizan Press, 1988), p.135.

Northampton's regiment until he was made prisoner at Compton House in 1644. This trooper presumably died of wounds sustained at Middleton Cheney and had been carried back to Banbury. Had he been slain during the battle, he would likely have been buried the next day in Middleton Cheney with the other dead.

Fig. 20 All Saints Church, Middleton Cheney, where some of those killed in the battle were interred in the churchyard.
(Author's Photograph)

The villagers of Middleton Cheney interred 46 soldiers in the churchyard, which is confirmed in the parish burial register.[5] These were presumably the slain left on the field and may have included the three Royalists. The register fails to record the allegiance of the soldiers and is only the briefest of entries. The 20th century war memorial is reputed to be the site of the grave, although this is not certain. Also, there are several burials recorded in the burial register for Banbury in addition to the one mentioned above. An entry in the register records '*Two soldiars of the Parliamentary army*', and there is a further entry of a single soldier for 9 May.[6] Whilst these soldiers

---

[5] Northamptonshire Records Office *All Saints Church Parish Register, Middleton Cheney, 1643*
[6] *Baptism and Burial Register of Banbury*, p.238-39

were probably taken prisoner and later died of their wounds, the information contained within the entries is inconclusive.

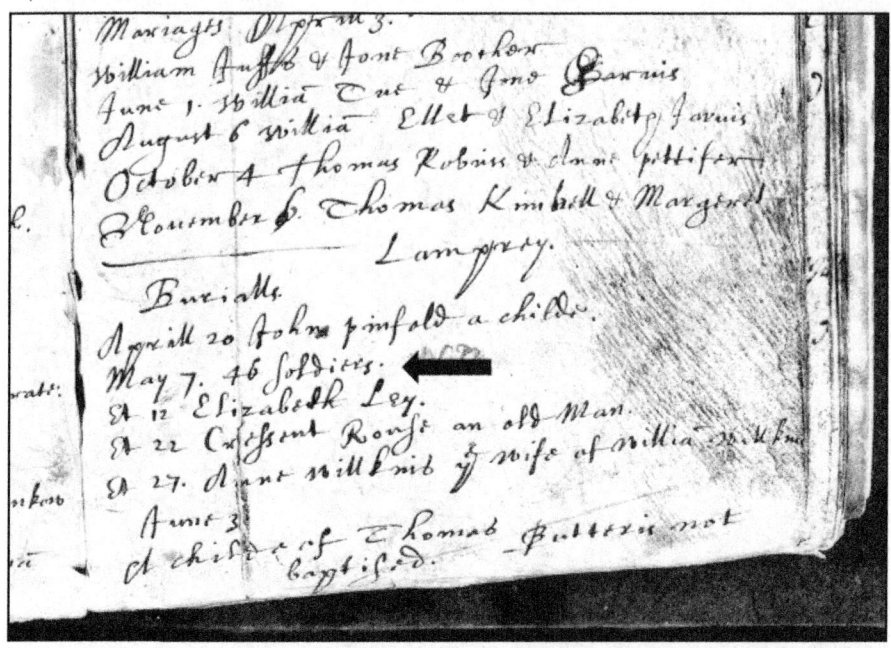

Fig. 21 The entry in the parish register showing the burial of 46 soldiers the day after the battle, currently in the Northamptonshire Records Office.
Photo: Nancy Long

The Earl of Northampton, as a punishment for the local support for the attack on Banbury:

'let the people of that County [Northamptonshire] *see the miserable effects of their disloyalty and disobedience, as to put them to the charge of tending, curing, and providing for their unfortunate party: his Lordship caused a great part of the wounded Prisoners, whom he had taken in the late fight, to be laid in Carts, and carried to some ill affected Villages of that County, and there left amongst them.'* [7]

Some soldiers might have been laid to rest locally if they succumbed to their wounds. Some of those who were able to return to Northampton may have died of their injuries. Whilst the Parliamentarian casualties were high, the Royalist accounts probably exaggerated the numbers to magnify the extent of their victory. Unless the

---
[7] *Mercurius Aulicus, The nineteenth Weeke,* Vol 1, p.265

Royalists were particularly ruthless in cutting down the fleeing Parliamentarian foot, the casualties are unlikely to have been as severe as the accounts suggest. Unlike the more significant battles fought during the war, other small-scale actions of a similar duration appear to have produced few casualties.[8]

The prisoners taken to Banbury were accommodated in different buildings. There are references to soldiers buried who were kept in the 'Towne hall', 'Leather Hall' and even in private houses. Many prisoners would not have stayed long in Banbury as the castle garrison would not have contained enough soldiers to guard them.[9] The Royalists would have kept those useful for a prisoner exchange and those too wounded to move. According to a pro-Parliament newspaper, some of the prisoners were cruelly treated. A week after the battle, many of the prisoners held in Banbury managed to escape:

> *'Many of the poore men that were prisoners in Banbury, are happily escaped, and got away, little less than sixtie in one night, their keepers (as was informed) being then drunke; and these prisoners have reveal'd such inhumane cruelties of the Cavaliers as would make even a souldiers heart tremble...they so cruelly handled them, that to some, they gave six wounds, to others seven or eight, nay to some of them ten or twelve.'*[10]

Whether this happened as narrated is unclear, although both sides did commit brutal acts and even massacres as the war continued. Whether any of the men who escaped were survivors from Middleton Cheney is unknown.

Whilst prisoners were valuable, capturing large quantities of arms, ammunition and provisions was also beneficial as they could be used by the Royalists to arm their own men. According to *Mercurius Aulicus,* the Royalists captured 416 Muskets, 150 pikes, 500 swords, the drake, and all the ammunition. Philip Willoughby wrote that Northampton's men *'took the cannon, all the ammunition, as many arms gathered up as four carts could bring.'*[11] Some of the Parliamentarian sources corroborate this as *A Continuation* reported that when they *'were put to flight, most of them left there Armes behind them'.*[12] Once again, most of the London newspapers differ from the Royalists' accounts. One talks of only 80 arms captured, although it admits that the

---

[8] The battle of Chalgrove Field fought on 18 June was a larger affair which produced estimates from 29-50 dead and more wounded. *His highnesse prince Ruperts late beating up the rebels quarters at Post-comb & Chinner in Oxfordshire. Also his victory in Chalgrove Field. Whereunto is added sr. Iohn Urries expedition to West-Wickham.* (Oxford, Leon Lichfield, 1643), Bodleian Library. Transcript at: https://johnhampdensregiment.org.uk/LateBeatingUp/#p=1 [Accessed: 7 October 2020]

[9] In 1644 the Royalists put captured Parliamentarians 'into a barn at Banbury', except for a clerk, who was held in the castle. Beesley, p.356

[10] *Special Passages Numb, 41.* (BL/TT/E.247(27).

[11] *Mercurius Aulicus, The Eighteenth Weeke,* Vol 1, p.257. Warburton, *Vol.II,* p.186.

[12] *A Continuation of certain Speciall and Remarkable Passages, from Thursday the 6. of May, till Thursday the 11. of May, 1643,* (Leach & Coles), (BL/TT/E.101(17).

Parliamentarians lost '*one Drake, a Carriage of Ammunition, and other provision*' whilst another speaks of 300 captured arms.[13] These would undoubtedly have been useful in helping equip further recruits and would also help replenish the supplies of the garrison in the castle. The victory at Middleton Cheney also appears to have increased recruitment for the Earl of Northampton's regiment:

> *'It was also certified this day, that the defeat given to the Rebels on Saturday last by the Earle of Northampton, had wrought so much upon the gentry of Northamptonshire...they had already sent him 80 Horse, and had undertaken also to raise two Troopes of Horse more, and 200 Dragooners'.* [14]

As Northamptonshire mostly supported Parliament, it is unclear how many of the promised Royalist recruits arrived.

Shortly after the battle, the long-awaited munitions convoy from the north arrived and was conveyed safely to Woodstock. Once Northampton completed his assignment, his command dispersed. He soon returned to Banbury with his regiment, presumably to complete its recruitment. The Prince's regiment went to Oxford to join Prince Rupert and fought at Chalgrove Field. The Banbury Royalists were soon engaged in minor raiding in Northamptonshire and the surrounding area again. The King himself lodged at Banbury while on his way to rendezvous with the Queen. Once she was safe in Oxford, his army re-supplied by the munitions convoy and following the defeat of a western Parliamentarian force at Roundway Down in mid-July, the King decided to take the offensive. Prince Rupert led an army which stormed Bristol on 23 July, after which the King decided to lay siege to Gloucester. By late August, the Banbury forces were again in action in a series of skirmishes against the Earl of Essex's army, which was marching to the relief of the besieged city. Northampton's regiment re-joined the army and fought at the first battle of Newbury (20 September), thus ending its operations in the Banbury area for the remainder of the year.

Although the Royalists appeared to have won a stunning victory at Middleton Cheney, what were the effects of the battle locally and within the national context? Did the battle contribute to a broader Royalist success and dominance in the central Midlands? Unfortunately for the Royalists, the answer is that it did not. The battle certainly did not change the strategic situation. The Parliamentarians still held their string of garrisons at Northampton, Coventry, Warwick and Stratford, which were to remain in their hands until the war's end. Locally, although weakened, Berkley's Northampton garrison regiment continued to exist. Despite it being an embarrassing defeat for Parliament, the battle neither failed to alter the strategic situation for the Royalists in the midlands nor weaken the local Parliamentarian forces to such an extent that they would cease to become a threat in the future.

---

[13] *Certaine Informations*, Numb.17, E.101(24). *A Perfect Diurnall* Numb.48, (BL/TT/E.249(6).
[14] *Mercurius Aulicus, The nineteenth Weeke,* Vol 1, p.265.

But what were the Parliamentarians attempting to accomplish by attacking Banbury? The capture of the town and castle and the destruction of a strong Royalist garrison would undoubtedly have been a significant coup. However, unless their intelligence system was faulty, the local committee must have received word of the convoy and its escort moving towards Banbury. With the flurry of activity in the north midlands, did they fail to notice the concentration of Royalist troops? It is also questionable whether the Parliamentarian force was ever a real threat to the munitions convoy. Once the Earl, Lord Percy and Henry Hastings, who commanded the convoy, had temporarily combined their commands, the Parliamentarians would have withdrawn without risking a battle which they would have had no hope of winning.

The most plausible answer to the question is that, from the Parliamentarian point of view, the neutralising of the Banbury garrison was a high priority for the Northamptonshire Committee. Ideally the Parliamentarians would have wished to install their own garrison in the castle to assist in the capture of Oxford. Was this, however, a realistic objective in May 1643? Would 700 men have been able to accomplish what a larger force with greater resources failed to do during the siege on 1644? Since the Parliamentarians were never in a position to threaten either the town or castle then this is something of a moot point. Even if the Committee was determined to occupy Banbury then the timing of the attack was surely opportunistic. The confusion resulting from the fire on 3 May was an opportunity not to be missed, and the chance to occupy Banbury, even temporarily, and capture the garrison was presumably a risk worth taking. Even if they had captured the town, it is doubtful if they would have been able to hold it for long enough to have pulled down the castle given the number of Royalist troops pouring into the Banbury area.

There are unanswered questions about the battle of Middleton Cheney which reflect the limited sources, and their widely differing accounts of events. There is the potential that the Bicester (or Claydon) skirmish has muddled some Parliamentarian accounts, which has confused the narrative and the gaps in the different reports also require us to use some conjecture to work out the course of events. Finally, the lack topographical details, which prevent the battle site from being accurately located from just the written sources. However, by looking at the tactics and the terrain, it has been possible to suggest the general area where the fighting is likely to have been located.

Overall, the immediate effects and longer-term strategic outcomes of the battle of Middleton Cheney were negligible and made little difference to the positions of either side. There were no territorial exchanges, and it did not neutralise the threat from each side's respective towns. Moreover, the Royalists failed to remove the danger from the Parliamentarian garrison at Northampton, and victory did not strengthen their position in the Midlands. The battle, however, adds to the story of the Civil War in Northamptonshire, which deserves recognition.

Appendix - Extracts from Primary Sources

Royalist

Philip Willoughby to Prince Rupert

May IT PLEASE YOUR HIGHNESS,
    I have received a command from my Lord of Northampton to have waited on your Highness if you were in town, if elsewhere to dispatch one presently to attend your Highness with an account of his yesterday's action; there came towards Banbury from Northampton four troops of horse, six or seven hundred foot, one piece of cannon of six pound bullet, all which came within half a mile of the town of Banbury. My Lord having only thirteen troops of horse with him, resolved to charge them, in which it hath pleased God that my Lord hath taken three hundred prisoners, killed above a hundred in the place, wounded most of the rest, took the cannon, all the ammunition, as many arms gathered up as four carts could bring, all which is in Banbury; all the foot officers taken or slain, but the horse as usually, made haste away, yet many of them came short home: my Lord lost not of all his company above three men, so, humbly taking leave, I rest, Sir,
    Your Highness's most humble servant,

Philip Willoughby.
Oxford, 7th May, 1643,
7 o'clock in the morning.

(Warburton, Memoirs of Prince Rupert, Vol.II, p.186)

Edward Hyde, 1st Earl of Clarendon

    Whilst both parties lay quiet, the one about Reading, the other about Abingdon or Oxford, without attempting one upon the other, or any action, save some small enterprises by parties (in which the King got advantage); as the young Earl of Northampton fortunately encountered a party of horse and foot from Northampton, which thought themselves strong enough to attempt upon Banbury : and having routed their horse killed above two hundred of their foot, and took as many more prisoners, most whereof were shrewdly hurt, the young Earl that day sacrificing to the memory of his father...

(Clarendon, Edward, Earl of, The History of the Rebellion and Civil Wars in England, p.388)

Mercurius Aulicus
(Ed. John Birkenhead/Peter Heylin)

The eighteenth Weeke

SATURDAY. May 6.

This night came a messenger with an Expresse from Banbury to Oxford, declaring what an absolute victory it pleased God to grant the Earle of Northampton over the Rebels at Middleton Cheney, not farre from Banbury; the particulars thus. About twelve of the clock to day my Lord had certaine notice of the Rebells being at Culworth, whereupon my Lord drew out his forces towards Bodicot within a mile of Banbury, where he saw the Enemy (being about 700 Foot and 4 or 5 troops of Horse) on the other side of the River; his Lordship sent a party commanded by Cap. Trist to face them, and keep them in action; which the Cap. Performed so well & souldierlike that he put the enemy into a posture of retreatings then my Lord drew up all his Horse being about 10 or 12 troops (for his Regiment of Foot was at the Leaguer) & found the enemy in a close body of Middleton Cheney Towne Field, where they made a stand & gave fire upon his Lordship : with their brasse peece 3 severall times, & then gave him a very hot volley of musket shot : which done His Lordship charged them on the front, Sergeant Major Daniel on the right wing, & Cap. Trist on the left : some of my Lords horse pursued theirs, killed and tooke many of them, yet the rest were so fleet that they escaped in small companies into by-lanes and hedges and ranne to Northampton to tell the news to their Brethren. But to avoid former errours of overhasty pursuing their fugitive horse, his Lordship charged their foot, & wholly routed them, killed 217
upon the place and tooke above 300 prisoners, tooke their brasse peece, 416 muskets, 150 pikes, and almost 500 swords : his Lordship lost but 3 men and none of any note, nor any officer so much as hurt save onely Major Daniell had a slight hurt in the Legge, the prisoners that were taken say they were commanded to march towards Banbury by the Committee, which as farre as we can gather was upon some treachery to be practiced on Banbury Towne and Castle being my Lords quarters, for there were Banbury men amongst these Rebels, & many of them lay dead in the field, there were divers Captaines and commanders taken, Captaine Martin, Captaine Melvin a Scottish man, with others whom we shall know better tomorrow when they are examined.

(Mercurius Aulicus; Communicating the Intelligence and affaires of the Court, to the rest of the kingdome, p.257)

The nineteenth Weeke

TUESDAY. May 9.

And it was signified withall, that as well to let the people of that County [Northamptonshire] see the miserable effects of their disloyalty and disobedience, as to put them to the charge of tending, curing, and providing for their unfortunate party : his Lordship caused a great part of the wounded Prisoners, whom he had taken in the late fight, to be laid in Carts, and carried to some ill affected Villages of that County, and there left amongst them.

Mercurius Aulicus; Communicating the Intelligence and affaires of the Court, to the rest of the kingdome, p.265).

The twentieth Weeke.

SATURDAY. May 20.

That the defeat given to the Rebels of Northamptonshire, not farre from Banbury, (whereof you heard a fortnight since) was by the counterfeiting of a Warrant under his Excellencies hand, commanding the 500 Foot that were in Northampton, to meet his Forces at Banbury, who comming out according unto that command, perfidiously were set upon by the Cavaliers ; which as it is unquestionably false, (the Rebels comming on in hope to have the Towne betrayed unto them by some of those faithfull men of Banbury) were it true, the greater fooles were they to be so deceived.

(Mercurius Aulicus; Communicating the Intelligence and affaires of the Court, to the rest of the kingdome, pg.289).

oooOOOooo

Parliamentarian

Mercurius Civicus

Numb. 1, 4th-11th May 1643

It was generally reported also Tuesday, May 9 that there were some of the Northampton Forces surprised by the Cavaliers that billeted in Banbury, they did after this manner, A warrant was framed by the Cavaliers, counterfeiting his Excellencies the Earle of Essex his hand, and sent to Northampton, commanding those 500 Foot that were there, to meet his Forces at Banbury, which according they intended to doe, but were most perfidiously set upon by the way, by the Cavaliers, who have taken and slaine many of them, which though it should prove true which seldome any of the malignants words doe,...

(Mercurius Civicus, London's Intelligencer, Volume I, 4th May-28th Dec 1643, p.12)

A Continuation of Certain Speciall and Remarkable Passages
(Cooke & Wood)

Numb. 44: From Thursday the 4. of May, till Thursday the 11. of the same, 1643

Out of Buckinghamshire it is certified this second of May, that whereas part of the Kings forces (after their returne from Redding to Oxford) came againe to Brill where before they were quartered, and finding their workes were demolished (as well by warrant given from Collonel Boulstrad who is at Ailsbury, as by their owne order when they went from thence) they stayed there but one night, and the next day marched to a towne about five miles from thence called Biscester, which place they have fortified, and that whereas Captiane Sayer was quartered at Clayden about 6 or 8 miles beyond Ailsbury, some of his scouts were taken by the Kings forces, and the said Captiane Sayer and Captaine Martine marched forth with their Troops (being Bedfordshire men) thinking to rescue their scouts, 3 or 4 Troops of the Kings forces which came from Banbury or thereabouts, fell upon them suddaynly, about 30 were slayne on both sides, and divers taken prisoners, and the said Captaine Sayer and Captaine Martine are thought to be either killed or taken prisoners, for they are wanting, and although I love to speak the truth, let it be on what side it will, yet least any malevolent tongues should boast of this great overthrow given to the Parliaments forces, I must crave leave likewise to be playne in relating other truthes that were informed the same day, viz.

(A Continuation of Certain Speciall and Remarkable Passages from both Houses of Parliament, and other Parts of the Kingdom, BL/TT/E,249(4))

A Continuation of Certain Speciall and Remarkable Passages
(Coles & Leach)

Numb. 44: From Thursday the 6. of May, till Thursday the 11. of May. 1643.

Letters from Northampton shire certify that the Northamptonshire men were so much incenced at the cruelty of the Cavaliers at Banbury in firing the Towne in their coole blood when no enemy approached it, but out of a devilish spite to the Towne, that they were not so forward to joyne in Compliance in their detestable and wicked courses, as they expected, but were in hopes to be free of the cruelty under which they have a long time groned, but their cruell oppressors since they intended to leave them , that the Towne might hereafter be unserviceable for any others fireing it intending onely to keepe a Garrison in the Castle, but the Northampton forces looking upon the same with much indignation resolved once more to trie their utmost to releive the oppressed inhabitants of Banbury and be revenged on the cruell Cavaliers, and to that purpose advanced with about five or 600 men & one smale Drake towards Banbury on Friday last, but before they could obtaine the Towne they were surprized by a great party of the enemyes Horse who were of two great powere to be opposed by so smale a force comeing on them with great advantage where by the Northampton forces were put to flight most of them left there Armes behind them, some killed and many taken prisoners, but the severall particulars of the overthrow of any certainty is not as yet informed.

(A Continuation of Certain Speciall and Remarkable passages informed to both Houses of Parliament, and otherwise from divers parts of this Kingdome, BL/TT/E.101(7))

A Perfect Diurnall
(Coles & Leach)

Numb. 48: From Munday the 8. of May till Munday the 15. of May.

By Letters out of Northamptonshire it is thus informed that the Cavaliers fained a letter from the Lord Generall. As though he should desire them, to fall on Banbury at such a time, when he would fall on Oxford, they received the letter but detained not the Messenger, and so according to the letter marched out towards Banbury about 600. strong, with one Canoneer which carryed a Drake, he that commanded in chiefe, had intelligence of three Ambuscadoes of horse in his March, and therefore commanded a retreat, but the Countrey people complayning of their being drawne out heretofore and had lost their labour, did

resolve to do somewhat before they would returne, well they went on according to their resolution, and beat up the first Ambuscado who fled to the second Ambuscardo, and there ralling themselves into one body charged our men, at which charge all our Horse ranne away, and so at the second charge the foote were routed and every man shifted for himselfe, the Cannonier shot three shot with his Drake, and killed of their men about 30. and unhorsed a gallant Sparke whom men suppose to be the Young Earle of Northampton, they slew of our men about 20. and took a 100. and odde of prisoners, for there are so many missing and 3. Captaines and 300. Armes.

(A Perfect Diurnall of the Passages in Parliament, BL/TT/E.249(6))

A Perfect Diurnall
(Cooke & Wood)

Numb. 49: From the 8. of May to the 15. of May.

This day information was given by letters out of Northamptonshire, that since the Cavaliers had fired and burnt down a great part of Banbury, about 100 houses, there was a great fight between the Kings forces that were about Banbury, some of them being quartered at Northampton, and others of them in the lower part of Buckinghamshire, the Parliaments forces consisting of about 500. horse and Dragoones, and some Foot, under the command of Captain Martin, Captain Needham, and Captain Sawyer, some report that the occasion of the Parliaments forces marching at this time was by reason of a counterfeit letter which was sent unto them from Prince Rupert, in his Excellencies name (the Earle of Essex) commanding them to come with their forces to Reading, others say they intended to be revenged on the Cavaliers for burning Banbury, but the first report is affirmed to be true by those that were there, and it is the more to be credited, for this is certain, that the Kings forces had provided for their coming, and had strengthened themselves, and lay in ambuscado in the way they were to march, and by cutting of their Scouts, they fell upon the Parliaments Forces suddenly, slew about 50. and took 300. Prisoners, and it was thought Captain Sawyer was killed, and two other Captains taken prisoners.

(A Perfect Diurnall of the Passages in Parliament, BL/TT/E.249(5))

Certaine Informations

Numb. 17: From the 8. of May to the 15. of May. 1643.

From Northampton they write, that a Gentleman came lately to their town with a Letter (which since hath proved forged) from the Parliaments Lord Generall, to require them to arme some horse and foot, and to send them to Banbury, where some of his forces should meet them, to drive the Cavaliers from thence ; whereunto they simply giving credit, presently sent out thither 500. horse and foot whither being come, they were presently surrounded with multitudes of horse from the towne, and miserably both cheated and defeated, insomuch that forty of them lost their lives, being slaine by the Cavaliers, sixty of them were taken prisoners, and they lost also eighty Armes, one Drake, and a Carriage of Ammunition and other provision, which happened unto them by their incautious credullty, yet their enemies lost some of their men also so that they have gotten bargaine by their treacherous stratagen.

(Certaine Informations From severall parts of the Kingdome, for the better satisfaction of all such who desire to be truly Informed of every weekes Passage, BL/TT/E.101(24))

The Kingdomes Weekly Intelligencer

Numb. 19: From Tuesday the 9. of May, to Tuesday the 15. of May. 1643.

As the Northampton Forces received a losse nere Banbury, both of men and Armes, so elsewhere the Parliaments Souldiers have regained a greater booty.

(The Kingdomes Weekly Intelligencer: SENT ABROAD to prevent mis-information, BL/TT/E.101(22)

The Speciall Passages
No.40

Another account is that 150 foot were sent on Thursday, as many on Friday, and three troops of horse about 120 in all, the whole commanded by the serjeant-major of Colonel Barkley. On a hill three miles from Banbury they saw troops coming, when the serjeant-major , contrary to the opinion of others, ordered his forces to descend into the valley , where they were defeated , and lost their drake and a load of match , powder, and bullet.

(Summarisation of the Special Passages, No.40 (Now lost) by Alfred Beesley in his History of Banbury)

Bibliography

Contemporary Sources

British Library

Harleian MS 6851. f.237v.

Add. MSS 18980 f20

Exact and Full Relation of all the Proceedings between the Cavaliers and the Northamptonshire forces at Banbury. (TT/E.84(10), London, 1642

The Earle of Portlands Charge, Being the relation of the Earle of Northamptons surprizing the Magazine at Banbury by the forging of a false Letter. (TT/E.110(8), London, 1642

A Perfect Diurnall of the Passages in Parliament, Numb. 47, (Frances Coles & Robert Leach), (TT/E.249(2), London, 1643

A Perfect Diurnall of the Passages in Parliament, Numb. 48, (Frances Coles & Robert Leach), (TT/E.249(6), London, 1643

A Perfect Diurnall of the Passages in Parliament, Numb. 49, (Walt. Cooke & Robert Wood), (TT/E.249(5), London, 1643

A Perfect Relation of the Cause and Manner of the Apprehending, by the Kings Souldiers, William Needle and Mistris Phillips, (TT/E.247(13), London, 1643

Anonymous, *The Latest intelligence of Prince Ruperts proceeding in Northamption-Shire and also Colonell Goodwins at Brill : both express in two letters / from hands of good Quality.* (London, 1642), (Wing/L563)

Certaine Informations from severall parts of the Kingdome, Num.17, (TT/E.101(4), London, 1643

The Kingdomes Weekly Intelligencer, Numb. 19, (TT/E.101(22). London, 1643

Speciall Passages And certain Informations from severall places, Collected for the use of all that desire to be truely informed, Numb, 39. (TT/E.101(6), London, 1643

Speciall Passages And certain Informations from severall places, Collected for the use of all that desire to be truely informed, Numb, 41. (TT/E.247(27), London, 1643

The Battaile on Hopton Heath in Staffordshire Betweene His Majesties Forces under the Right Honourable the Earle of Northampton and those Rebels, March 19 (Oxford, H.Hall, 1643), (TT/E.99(18)

A Continuation of Certaine Speciall and Remarkable Passages from both Houses of Parliament, and other Parts of the Kingdom. From Thursday the 4. of May. till Thursday the 11. of the same, 1643, Numb. 44. (Walt. Cooke & Robert Wood), (TT/E.249(4), London, 1643.

A Continuation of certain Speciall and Remarkable Passages informed to both Houses of PARLIAMENT and otherwise from divers part of the Kingdome, From Thursday the 6. of May, till Thursday the 11. of May, 1643, (Leach & Coles), (TT/E.101(17), London, 1643.

A full Relation of the Siege of Banbury Castle by that Valiant and Faithfull Commander, Colonell Whetham, Governour of Northampton, now Commander-in-Chiefe in that Service, &c. (TT/E.8(9), London, 4 September, 1644

Mercurius Britanicus, communicating the affaires of great Britaine for the better information of the people, Numb.70. (TT/E.269 (25), London, 10 February 1645

Corbert, John, *A true and impartiall History of the Military Government of the Citie of Gloucester,* (Printed for R. Bostock, London, Pauls Church-yard, 1647), (TT/E.402(4)

Others

Bulstrode, Sir Richard, *Memoirs and Reflections upon the Reign and Government of King Charles the Ist and King Charles IId.* (London: Printed by N.Mist, for Charles Rivington, at the Bible and Crown in St.Pauls Churchyard, 1721)

Calendar of the Proceedings of the Committee for Compounding, &c., 1643-1660: Cases, 1643-1646, (Ed. Mary Anne Everett Green), (London, HMSO, 1890)

Clarendon, Edward Hyde, 1st Earl of, *The History of the Rebellion and Civil Wars in England,* (Oxford, Oxford University Press, 1843)

Gibson, J.S.W. (ed) *Baptism and Burial Register of Banbury, Oxfordshire, Part One, 1558-1653,* (Oxford, The Banbury Historical Society Vol.7, 1966)

Heath, James, *A Chronicle of the Late Intestine War in the Three Kingdoms of England, Scotland and Ireland, With the Intervening Affairs of Treaties, and Other Occurrences Relating Thereunto. As Also the Several Usurpations, Forreign Wars, Differences and Interests Depending Upon It, to the Happy Restitution of Our Sacred Soveraign K. Charles II. In Four Parts, Viz. The Commons War, Democracie, Protectorate, Restitution* (Printed by J.E, for Thomas Basset, at the George, Cliffords-Inn in Fleetstreet, London, 1676)

House of Lords Parliamentary Office, HL/PO/JO/10/1/265, 25/7/1648.

Jones, S.F (ed) *Indigent Officers; Civil War Officers Rewarded by Charles II, The 1663 Indigent Officers List Transcribed and Indexed,* (Tygers Head Books, 2015)

Journal of the House of Lords, Volume IV, Charles I, 1625-1642, (No date or publisher)

Marsh, Simon *The Train of Artillery of the Earl of Essex; The Accounts of Sir Edward Peyto, Lieutenant General to the Train of Artillery, October 1642-September 1643,* (Romford, The Pike & Shot Society, 2016)

Mercurius Aulicus; Communicating the Intelligence and affaires of the Court, to the rest of the kingdome, The English Revolution III, Newsbooks I, Oxford royalist, Volume 2. Ed. by Robin Jeffs et al., (London: Cornmarket Press, 1971)

Mercurius Aulicus; Communicating the Intelligence and affaires of the Court, to the rest of the kingdome, The English Revolution III, Newsbooks I, Oxford royalist, Volume 3. Ed. by Robin Jeffs et al., (London: Cornmarket Press, 1971)

Mercurius Civicus: London's Intelligencer, Volume I, 4th May - 28th December 1643. Ed. Jones, S.F. (Tygers Head Books, 2013)

Northamptonshire Records Office *All Saints Church Parish Register, Middleton Cheney, 1643*

The National Archives, - SP28/10 f.259-60
- SP28/18 f.31
- SP28/262 f.186
- PROB 11/342/687
- SP28/238 v.1 f.59
- SP28/238 v.2 f.569
- SP28/238 v.4 f. 591, 596, 599, 601, 602,603, 627, 633, 640, 686

Philip, I.G. (ed), *Journal of Sir Samuel Luke,* (Banbury: Cheney & Sons, 1950)

Walker (Sir), E. *Historical Discourses upon Several Occasions.* Ed. by H. Clapton. (London: Printed for Samuel Keble, 1705).

Secondary Sources

Ashley, Maurice, T*he English Civil War,* (London: Thames and Hudson, 1974)

Ashton, Robert, *Counter Revolution, The Second Civil War and its Origins, 1646-8,* (Avon, The Bath Press, 1994)

Beesley, Alfred, *The History of Banbury: Including Copious Historical and Antiquarian Notices of the Neighborhood,* (London, Nichols and Son, 1841)

Blackmore, David, *Arms and Armour of the English Civil Wars,* (London, Royal Armouries, 1990)

Brooks, Richard, *Cassells Battlefield of Britain and Ireland,* (London, Weidenfeld & Nicholson, 2005)

Brown, M.W., M.A. *Northamptonshire* (Cambridge County Geographies), (Cambridge, University Press, 1911)

Brzezinski, Richard, *Lützen 1632: Climax of the Thirty Years Wa*r, (Oxford, Osprey Publishing, 2001)

Bull, Stephen, *The Furie of the Ordnance; Artillery in the English Civil Wars,* (Woodbridge, The Boydell Press, 2008)

Evans, Graham, *The Battle of Edgcote 1469 - Re-evaluating the evidence,* (Northampton Battlefields Society, 2019)

Frank, Joseph, *The Beginnings of the English Newspaper, 1620-1660,* (Cambridge, Harvard University Press, 1961)

Henry, Chris, *English Civil War Artillery 1642-51,* (Oxford, Osprey Publishing Ltd, 2005)

Jerrams, Leonard W., *A Brief History of Middleton Cheney, Northamptonshire with Childhood Memories,* (1984)

Kelliher, Hilton, *A hitherto unrecognized cavalier dramatist: James Compton, third Earl of Northampton,* The British Library Journal, Vol. 6, No. 2 (AUTUMN 1980)

Kenyon, John, *The Civil Wars in England,* (London: Weidenfeld and Nicholson Ltd, 1988)

Leslie, Stephen (Ed.), *Dictionary of National Biography, Volume XIV, Damon-D'Eyncourt,* (London, Smith, Elder, & Co, 1888)

Lipscombe, Nick, *The English Civil War; An Atlas and concise history of the Wars of the Three Kingdoms 1639-51,* (Oxford, Osprey Publishing Ltd, 2020)

Marsh, Simon, *A Case of Drakes - James Wemyss and Artillery Innovations in the Civil Wars, A new way of fighting: Professionalism in the English Civil Wars,* (Solihull, Helion and Company Ltd, 2017)

Morris, Robert, *The Battle of Cropredy Bridge 1644,* (Bristol, Stuart Press, 1994)

Ollard, Richard, *This war without an enemy* (Fontana Paperbacks, 1992)

Ordnance Survey 6 inch to 1 mile Old Map (1888-1913) of Middleton Cheney, Northamptonshire.

Porter, Stephen & Marsh, Simon, *The Battle for London,* (Stroud, Amberley Publishing, 2011)

Reid, Stuart, *Officers and Regiments of the Royalist Army, Volume 3, I-Q,* (Newthorpe, Partizan Press, 1988)

Roberts, Keith, *Pike and Shot Tactics 1590-1660,* (Oxford, Osprey Publishing Ltd, 2010)

Roberts, Keith, *First Newbury 1643, The turning point,* (Oxford, Osprey Publishing Ltd, 2003)

Roberts, Keith & Tincey, John, *Edgehill 1642; First Battle of the English Civil War,* (Oxford, Osprey Publishing Ltd, 2001)

Royle, Trevor, *Civil War; The Wars of the Three Kingdoms 1638-1660,* (London, Abacus, 2005)

Sherwood, Roy, *The Civil War in the Midlands 1642-51,* (Stroud, Alan Sutton Publishing Ltd, 1992)

Tennant, Philip, *Edgehill and Beyond, The Peoples War in the South Midlands 1642-45,* (Stroud, Alan Sutton Publishing Ltd, 1992)
Tincey, John, *Soldiers of the English Civil War (2) Cavalry,* (Oxford, Osprey Publishing Ltd, 1990)
T*he Caracole : Is it Leading us Around in Circles?* Arquebusier : The Journal of the Pike and Shot Society, XXXVII/III, (Witney, Pike and Shot Society, 2020)
Thomas, P.W., *Sir John Berkenhead 1617-1679 A royalist Career in Politics and Polemics,* (Oxford, Clarendon Press, 1969)
Warburton, Eliot, *Memoirs of Prince Rupert, and the cavaliers, Vol.II* (London, Richard Bentley, 1849)
Wedgewood, C.V., *The Kings Peace,* (London, Book Club Associates, 1974)
Whellan & Co., William, *History, Gazetteer, and Directory of Northamptonshire; Comprising a general survey of the county,* (London, Whittaker and Co., 1749)
Young, Peter, *The Prince of Wales Regiment of Horse 1642-46* (Leeds, Raider Books, 1988)
The Cavalier Army; Its organisation and everyday life, (Chatham, George Allen & Unwin Ltd, 1974)

Online Sources

His highnesse prince Ruperts late beating up the rebels quarters at Post-comb & Chinner in Oxfordshire. Also his victory in Chalgrove Field. Whereunto is added sr. Iohn Urries expedition to West-Wickham. (Oxford, Leon Lichfield, 1643), Bodleian Library. Transcript at: https://johnhampdensregiment.org.uk/LateBeatingUp/#p=1 [Accessed: 7 October 2020]

'Surnames beginning 'S'', in The Cromwell Association Online Directory of parliamentarian Army Officers, ed. Stephen K Roberts (2017), British History Online http://www.british-history.ac.uk/no-series/cromwell-army-officers/surnames-s [accessed 20 October 2020].

'House of Lords Journal Volume 9: 1 May 1647', in Journal of the House of Lords: Volume 9, 1646 (London, 1767-1830), pp. 165-173. British History Online http://www.british-history.ac.uk/lords-jrnl/vol9/pp165-173 [accessed 21 October 2020].

Bellamy, Roger, *The Church of St. Peter and St. Paul, A Historical Guide. Church booklet:* https://www.kingssutton.org/static/content-uploads/pdfs/2013/07/22/Church_History_Final_Colour.pdf. [Accessed 20 November 2020].

'Middleton Cheney', in *An Inventory of the Historical Monuments in the County of Northamptonshire, Volume 4, Archaeological Sites in South-West Northamptonshire*

(London, 1982), pp. 101-102. British History Online http://www.british-history.ac.uk/rchme/northants/vol4/pp101-102 [accessed 8 January 2021].

BCW Regimental Page, parliamentarian, Foot Regiments. http://wiki.bcw-project.org/parliamentarian/foot-regiments/col.-david-berkley [accessed 4/10/21].

Commemorating the battle

In 2018 the Battlefields Trust was contacted by Middleton Cheney village resident Captain Nicholas Haynes RGJ (retd.) asking for assistance with a project he was leading to commemorate the Civil War battle that had been fought in the village in May 1643. The request was passed to the Trust's Mercia Region and, having done a small amount of research on the battle, I was dispatched to meet Nick to see how the Trust could assist. Nick was already working with the Parish Council and the local church in what was a project led by the village and local community. The Trust offered to assist with these efforts acting at an advisory level with myself taking the lead on the research of the battle whilst my regional co-chair, Simon Marsh, would design the planned information board and give advice on the project as a whole.

Sadly, Nick died in a tragic accident in 2021 and the project, which had been steadily progressing, came to an abrupt halt. After a hiatus of several months the Trust was contacted by Nick's widow, Ulrika, about completing the project in his memory. A partnership was formed including the Parish Council, Church of England and other local stakeholders. The project was also joined by the Northamptonshire Battlefields Society. The goals of the project were to complete the efforts already begun by Nick. This would see an interpretation board placed at the most likely site for the battle, a plaque commemorating the slain in the churchyard and a battlefield trail leaflet on the battle. A series of small events were planned, initially for the anniversary date on 6 May 2023. However, finding that we could not compete with another King Charles, who had scheduled his coronation for this date, the planned unveiling will now take place in early June. A battlefield survey is also planned to take place before the completion of the project.

Gregg Archer
January 2023

The Battlefields Trust

The Battlefields Trust is a volunteer run national charity dedicated to the preservation, research, and presentation of battlefields as historical and educational resources. It is interested in battlefields globally, but most of its work is focused within the UK.

The Trust monitors planning applications affecting battlefields and, where appropriate, argues against development or seeks mitigation of the plans to ensure the understanding of the battlefield and its archaeology are preserved as far as possible. It conducts research, including archaeological surveys, on battlefields and uses the results to better inform its interpretation and preservation efforts.

Through its online and in-person talks, walks, study days, and interpretation projects the Trust aims to better inform the public about the UK's rich battlefield heritage and why it is a vital resource that needs to be better understood and protected.

You can support this important work by becoming a member of the Battlefields Trust. Members receive a quarterly magazine, free access to our growing programme of walks and outstanding series of online talks by experts in their field. If you have some time to spare, we are also always on the look-out for volunteers who can assist in our work.

If you would like to learn more about the Trust or become a member please visit the Trust's website at www.battlefieldstrust.com or email info@battlefieldstrust.com.

Northamptonshire Battlefields Society

Northamptonshire Battlefields Society was formed in February 2014 in order to promote and preserve the county's battlefields heritage.

The Society brings together the local community, members of the public, historians, wargamers, archaeologists, re-enactors and academics from all over Britain, Europe and the US, but especially Northamptonshire, who all share a passion for Northamptonshire's rich but apparently largely forgotten history.

The Society holds 10 meetings a year, which take place at Delapré Abbey, Northampton, normally on the last Thursday of the month (excluding August and December). The Speaker Programme includes a wide range of high calibre expert speakers from all over the UK. Meetings are free to fully paid up NBS members or £5.00 to non-members on the door. Membership fees are £20 for a single member and £30 for a family (this is the charge as at 2023.).

The Society also takes a mobile exhibition stand to a number events around the country including major wargames shows, where you have a good chance of meeting the author. The Society's e-newsletter is published a quarterly. Called "The Wild Rat" (named after the banner that the men of Northampton marched under when they were summonsed to join a Royal Army) it reports on all of the regular meetings and keeps members up to date with issues of concern and the Society's activities.

Original research is a key part of the Society's purpose, and it has published books on the 1460 Battle of Northampton, the Battle of Edgcote, as well as a general history of the Battlefields of Northamptonshire. All these publications can be found for sale on Amazon worldwide.

Further information can be found at northantsbattles.com or through our Facebook page: https://www.facebook.com/groups/Northampton1460. You can contact the Society by email at northampton.battlefields@gmail.com

Printed in Great Britain
by Amazon

26863413R00056